The
CALLANDER and OBAN
RAILWAY

by
C.E.J. Fryer

THE OAKWOOD PRESS

© Oakwood Press and C.E.J. Fryer 1989

ISBN 0 85361 377 X

Typeset by Gem Publishing Company, Brightwell, Wallingford, Oxfordshire

Printed by Nuffield Press, Cowley, Oxford

Caledonian 0–6–0 "Jumbo" and Oban Bogie "Mark II" in L.M.S. livery, No. 14607
(formerly Caledonian No. 53), approaching Oban with an excursion train on 12th
June, 1927.   *H.C. Casserley*

Published by
The OAKWOOD PRESS
P.O. Box 122, Headington, Oxford

Contents

	Introduction	5
Chapter One	The Area Served	9
Chapter Two	Preliminaries to Construction	13
Chapter Three	Getting off to a Slow Start	17
Chapter Four	Advancing into Argyll	23
Chapter Five	The Project Accomplished	27
Chapter Six	The Route Described	31
Chapter Seven	Stations, Signalling and Permanent Way	65
Chapter Eight	The Killin Branch and the Unbuilt Branch to the Trossachs	75
Chapter Nine	The West Highland Connection and the Branch to Ballachulish	91
Chapter Ten	Locomotives and Rolling Stock: 1880–1965	115
Chapter Eleven	Passenger Train Services: 1880–1965	133
Chapter Twelve	Accidents and Mishaps	149
Chapter Thirteen	Partial Closure and the disused lines to-day	155
Chapter Fourteen	The Oban Branch: 1965 to the present day	161
	Appendix One: Principal Bridges on the Line	167
	Appendix Two: The automatic safety screen in the Pass of Brander	171
	Appendix Three: Mileages	172
	Appendix Four: Locomotive details	173
	Appendix Five: Principal events of the Callander and Oban Rly.	174
	Bibliography & Acknowledgements	175
	Index	176

The end of the line: Ballachulish Station in April 1952 with its interesting "Trespass Notice". Behind the Station Ballachulish slate quarry is visible. *H.C. Casserley*

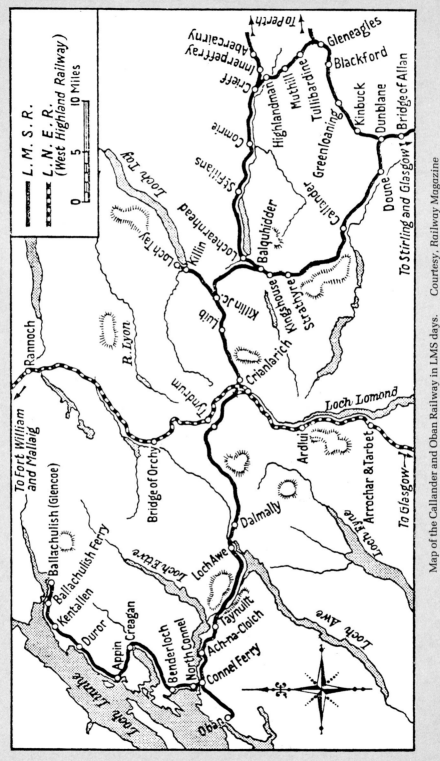

Map of the Callander and Oban Railway in LMS days.   Courtesy, Railway Magazine

Introduction

The coming of a railway to an area of outstanding natural beauty was not always a welcome event in the mid-nineteenth century. The poet Wordsworth, for example, took a very poor view of the proposal to link Windermere with the Lancaster and Carlisle line in 1844, and wrote an anguished sonnet beginning:

> Is then no nook of English ground secure
> From rash assault?

A railway, of all uncouth things, to pollute his beloved hills and vales! One wonders how he would have reacted to the nuclear plant at Sellafield, or to the innumerable motor vehicles which now invade his village and leave their fumes behind.

One can sympathise with his fear that the subtle beauties of this most scenic part of England might be marred by what he called a "false utilitarian lure". But how much does a railway damage an environment? One can imagine horrible things – a rack railway to the summit of Scafell Pike, for example, like the one up Snowdon. But it is surely not a question of whether at all, anywhere, but of how much and in what area. If one stands on the fellside in the Lune valley near Tebay one is scarcely aware of the railway, in spite of its electrified overhead wires, but very much aware of the M6. A landscape on a large scale can absorb even a main line railway, and if Wordsworth were living at this hour he would surely have agreed that a railway line spoils the landscape far less than a motorway.

When the Callander and Oban line made its way across the Central Highlands of Scotland, few regarded it as a deplorable intrusion, though some of the landowners jibbed at being able to see it from the windows of their mansions. Rural seclusion is all very well, but access to urban amenities is usually felt by the rurally secluded to be a good thing, and if moneyed tourists could also be persuaded to use the new route of access, so much the better. In mountain landscapes on the Scottish scale the environment is not spoiled; the railway merely becomes an unobtrusive part of it. The Central Highlands are huge, with hill-summits that soar far higher than any over which Wordsworth tramped in his native Cumbria; walking among them, one is almost glad to see the shining iron ribbons breaking the monotony of pinewoods, heather, grass and bracken.

Wordsworth came this way himself before the railway intruded, for he was a man of leisure, thanks to his possession of a Government sinecure which required practically no work from him in return. He travelled by horse-drawn carriage and relaxed against its cushions, wrapt in composition while his sister Dorothy took notes for her journal. He sheltered from a storm at Tyndrum, admired the rainbow that appeared between showers over Loch Etive, poured scorn on the owner of a caged eagle at Dunollie Castle "who kept the Bird of Jove embarred", and wrote verses about all of them. He took his time, since he could afford to. Coming after him, the engineers of the Callander and Oban Railway opened up this magnificent landscape for the benefit of those with scanter leisure than his, a mere week or two to spend between spells of work. Some come to walk – the best way for the young and vigorous; some bring their cycles; some scurry along in cars and do not see all they might. But for those who rode the whole length of the line by train, a thing now, alas, impossible, there was the more reflective pleasure of medi-

This view shows Oban Bay about 1890. The railway pier, station and North Pier can clearly be seen.　　　　　　　　　　　　　　　　　　　Courtesy, David and Charles

The restricted approach to Oban station and pier in 1880, showing the enormous signal cabin.　　　　　　　　　　　　　　　　　　Courtesy, David and Charles

tatively regarding banks and braes, bens and glens, through carriage windows and enjoying the many *coups d'oeil* as they came unexpectedly into sight. Thus the journey along the line became a genuine part of the holiday.

"Caledonia stern and wild" (as Sir Walter Scott called his native land) was later in receiving the railway than the Lake District. It was not until 1863 that the Scottish Central line, having reached Perth, put out a branch from Dunblane to Callander which remained for a short while like a finger pointing into the western mountains. Then the call came from Oban for a link to be made. In 1864 the decision was taken; Parliament approved and the navvies moved in. After a painfully slow advance from Callander, in four stages with lengthy halts between each, at an average rate of 0.00005 miles an hour (a reasonably active snail could have outstripped them) Oban was reached in July 1880. The whole line enjoyed eighty-five years of continuous use until falling receipts and falling rocks determined the fate of the easternmost three-sevenths, and what still remained became the Oban branch of the West Highland line. Altered, slimmed and deprived of two offshoots, it still remains the pleasantest way of travelling into the land of Lorne; the building of a new terminus at Oban and the re-opening of Loch Awe station suggest that its continuance is intended.

My own acquaintance with the line dates from 1954, when I bought as a holiday cottage the house where I now reside, right beside the junction where the spur from the West Highland line joins the route of the Callander and Oban half a mile west of where Crianlarich Lower station used to be. As a family we used the line frequently during school vacations, for shopping excursions to Stirling or Oban, for visiting friends at Killin, or for going to relax on the sands of Ardmucknish Bay near Benderloch, the first station along the line from Connel Ferry to Ballachulish. The whole line still had ten years before it as a going concern, and there were four trains a day in each direction, including a through sleeping car service from and to London. As I write memories return. There were the long waits at Killin Junction, a station to which no one ever took a ticket since it was merely the changing-place for Killin, which was reached by a funny little one coach train, of which more in one of the following chapters. There were the occasions when we had to run hard as we could along the road to Benderloch station, the two of us with a small daughter and one or perhaps two teddy bears, when the distant whistle of the engine on the branch line train told us we had only five minutes in which to catch it. There was the delight of eating high tea in the restaurant car on the evening train back from Oban – fish fried in bread crumbs disappearing in luscious mouthfuls as one gazed across the gleaming waters of Loch Awe.

After 1965 memories change. Diesels replaced the steam locomotives, cascaded Mark 1 coaches replaced old pre-war stock, trains no longer came from Stirling but were routed round the spur from Crianlarich Upper station on their way from Glasgow Queen Street. From and to Glasgow it became a better service, so far as the time taken was concerned, and no worse to Edinburgh despite having to change at Queen Street and travel 105 miles instead of 80. On the debit side of the account is the disappearance of the restaurant car; one can no longer eat in style; a very skimpy service of drinks and sandwiches is a poor replacement. But by and large the service is a good one and, making due allowance for inflation, one has to agree that it costs no more. There are also Sunday trains in each direction throughout the year. Better things still are promised when the Sprinters arrive. Reason approves, but nostalgia still hankers for the old days, for the sound of a "Black Five's" hooter echoing across Strathfillan, for the superb view from the window as the train toiled up to Glenoglehead and the whole of Loch Earn could be seen almost as if from an aircraft. We are probably lucky to have this rail link still for its closure has often been rumoured. Long may it continue.

C.E.J. Fryer. 1989

68.—CALLANDER AND OBAN.

Incorporated by 28 and 29 Vic.. cap. 266 (5th July, 1865), to construct a line from the town of Oban to the Dunblane Doune and Callander. Length, 70¾ miles. Capital, 600,000l. in shares, and 200,000l. on loan. Arrangements with Scottish Central (Caledonian), which subscribes 200,000l., and is to work the line at 50 per cent.

It was reported in September that a new agreement had been made with the Caledonian, to the effect, first, for a reduction from the nominal capital of 600,000l. The amount fixed by agreement being already subscribed, the company would be enabled to borrow one-third of the usual amount, thereby increasing the capital from 300,000l. to 325,500l. This capital, it was assumed, was sufficient to carry the line to Tyndrum. The agreement also provided for limitation of the line to Tyndrum ; and the Caledonian became bound to apply for Parliamentary sanction for including the agreement in the first bill they promoted. The only other change of importance was that the cost of working and maintenance, instead of being as originally provided, 50 per cent. of the gross receipts was to be limited to the actual cost price.

CAPITAL.—The receipts and expenditure on this account to 31st July, 1869, have been as follow :—

Received.		*Expended.*	
Shares	£193,439	On line in course of construction	£148,995
		Balance	45,143
	£193,439		£193,439

In the receipts on account of capital, there is included a sum of 32,000l. deposited in bank, being a portion of Parliamentary deposit receivable, and treated as a payment to account of calls.

No. of Directors—9 ; quorum, 3. *Qualification*, 500l.

DIRECTORS:

* Chairman—J. C. BOLTON, Esq., West George Street, Glasgow, and Carbrook, near Stirling.

* Deputy-Chairman—DANIEL AINSLIE, Esq.. 48, Moray Place, Edinburgh, and The Gart, Callander.

3 John Wingfield Malcolm, Esq.. M.P., Holm Lodge, Wimbledon, S.W., and Inverliver, Killinartin, Argyleshire.
1 Robert Mactie, Esq., of Airds, Fort William.
2 Captain Farquhar Campbell, of Aros, Mull.

2 Robert Tennant, Esq., Scarcroft Lodge, Leeds.
* James F. Wyllie, Esq., Bolfracks, Aberfeldy.
* John Wilson, Esq., Hill Park, Bannockburn.
* James Clerk, Esq., Park Circus, Glasgow.

* Represent the Caledonian. 1. Retire in 1870 ; 2. in 1871 ; 3, in 1872.

OFFICERS.—Sec., John Anderson ; Engs., B. and E. Blyth, Edinburgh ; Auditors, Henry Kerr and John Graham, Accountants, Glasgow ; Solicitors, Sheill and Small, Dundee.

Offices—48, Dundas Street, Glasgow.

Extract from *Bradshaw's Shareholders' Manual* of 1870.

Chapter One
The Area Served

A century and a quarter ago the Highlands of Scotland had not been opened up to tourists. Only one line had so far penetrated them – the Highland Railway, which linked Inverness with Perth by way of Forres, Dava Moor, Aviemore, Druimuachdar Pass, Pitlochry and Dunkeld. Elsewhere communications were poor. The principal roads along the valleys were narrow, scarcely wide enough for two horse-drawn carriages to pass, and in places steeply graded. If they were metalled it was roughly done; not all had tar-macadam surfaces; there were ruts and potholes. Had there been any cyclists in those days, they would have made better times from place to place than the toiling horses which needed to be changed at intervals. During the summer months private carriages might also be seen, conveying the few who had money and leisure to make sentimental journeys through a land of legend and romance. During the eighteenth century, after the two Jacobite rebellions had been successfully put down, the very un-sentimental Dr. Johnson had come this way with his young friend James Boswell, who enthused about the noble scenery and had his romantic notions prosaically corrected by his companion; the mountains, he was told, were no more than considerable protuberances.

Sir Walter Scott, however, coming somewhat later, regarded the "land of the mountain and the flood" with a very different eye and wrote novels in prose and verse about it and its peoples, so that the latter, once regarded with distaste as savage tribesmen disloyal to the House of Hanover, acquired an aura of romance and attracted sentimental admiration now that they had passed into history and their once-dangerous chieftains had been tamed, exiled or decapitated. Prince Charles, frequently urged in song to come back again, never did; returning into exile, he eventually drank himself to death. The descendants of those who had hunted him down came to admire the mountains among which he had skulked in hiding after the battle of Culloden, and shed a few tears over his gallant failure. Such earlier travellers took their time, staying with wealthy acquaintances or at the few sufficiently well-appointed inns, enduring the weather in the glens and admiring the heather on the bens from a safe distance.

The Scotland they visited was not at all the Scotland she had once been. Previous to the Jacobite rebellions the Highlanders had mostly been Catholics, but the old religion was now dying out except in pockets where old clan loyalties still lingered. Many of the upper classes were Episcopalians; the national Kirk and (since the celebrated "Disruption") the Free Church, claimed the rest; preaching, lengthy and often grim, took the place of the Mass. On a more mundane level, there had been something like an economic revolution, when existing property owners, with an eye for profits, had carried out the notorious "clearances", and poorer tenants had been evicted from their holdings and forced to emigrate, the alternative being starvation and perhaps having your roof burned over your head. Sheep replaced them; it was more lucrative to rear them and cash in on their fleeces than to collect small rents from the peasantry. The uncultivable higher ground was given over to deer and grouse, preserved so that the landowners and their friends could enjoy a season's sport. Empty houses, roofless and nettle-grown, showed the extent of the depopulation. Those still inhabited were strung out along the straths and glens, with clusters here and there in villages which sometimes attained the dignity, in fact if not in name, of small market towns. Large areas of the country were owned by wealthy and often titled land-owners such as the Marquess of Breadalbane, whose estates extended from Aberfeldy to the Firth of Lorne. They rented portions to tenants through their factors, and these latter kept a watchful eye on the former in defence of their master's interests. If a family became too numerous there was always the safety valve of emigration. Spare sons might enlist in the Army, and domestic service absorbed daughters.

The landed proprietors were not always Scots; much land was bought by newcomers from England. A large part of Strathfillan once belonged to a wealthy immigrant from Yorkshire, a certain Francis Place (not to be con-fused with the nineteenth century political reformer of the same name) who resided in Loch Dochart Lodge and owned land on either side of Crianlarich. His descendants have now utterly vanished from the scene, having ruined themselves with mutual litigation; there were, I am afraid, many dry eyes among those who contemplated their misfortunes, for the family was not popular and in their day behaved rather oppressively. Wally Campbell, an old signalman who operated the frame in Crianlarich East signal box in 1954, told me of an incident from his childhood, when the Place's factor des-cended one day on the humble dwelling of one of his master's tenants who was suspected of having helped himself to a deer. No sign of any carcass could be found, nor did any joints hang from the ceiling, but the factor recognized the smell of venison cooking in a pot over the kitchen fire. This was sufficient evidence and the tenant and his family were evicted. Some-thing of the old resentment felt by the lower orders came out in the manner in which the signalman told his tale. This must have happened quite late in the nineteenth century, after the Callander and Oban line was already oper-ating and doing its part to blur the old semi-feudal distinctions.

The land of Breadalbane and the tracts adjoining it to the south-east and to the west, across which the new line was to pass, were sparsely populated regions which could not of themselves be expected to generate much custom. The hills are high; travelling by train between Callander and Oban one could sight on a clear day as many as twenty Munros (summits over 3,000 feet in altitude) which is more than can be found in England, Wales and Ireland taken together. The main valleys between them are quite deep; between Callander and Oban it is nowhere necessary to rise as much as a thousand feet above sea-level, whether by road or rail. The country is rugged and boulder-strewn, though nowhere very precipitous. An average winter will provide coverings of snow on Ben More and Stobinian (to name but two of the principal heights) to tempt ski-ers and winter climbers, and attract, too, the insufficiently-trained or improperly equipped; Ben More claims at least one life each year. The lower slopes of the hills were bare when the line was first built; afforestation has now clothed many of them with pines, larches and spruces. In the glens animals are reared, and there is a herd of Highland cattle in Glen Dochart; motorists from the south, seeing them, can scarcely believe their eyes, stop their cars and get out their cameras. Small lochs here and there diversify the landscape. There are some attractive ruins, notably Kilchurn Castle on a low peninsula which juts out into the north-eastern end of Loch Awe.

The railway passes within stone-throwing distance of the sites of two bloody mediaeval clan fights in which Robert the Bruce took part – Dalrigh in upper Strathfillan and the Pass of Brander. It skirts the northern shore of Loch Awe, one of the largest sheets of fresh water in Scotland, reputed once to have had a monster of its own like Loch Ness, though no reports of its presence have appeared in living memory. Finally it runs along the southern shore of Loch Etive as far as the narrow strait which separates the latter from the Firth of Lorne. Generally speaking the scenery is reminiscent of the English Lake District as far as Lochearnhead; it becomes bleaker and more austere as Glen Ogle is climbed, displays a wide magnificence along the valleys of the Dochart, Fillan and Lochy, is very picturesque as far as Bridge of Awe, and for the rest of the way to Oban is broken, varied and charming, affording long vistas towards Morven and Mull.

It was not the desire to open these grandeurs to visitors, however, which led to the proposal to build a railway through them. The initiative came from the far end of the route, from the townsfolk of Oban: from that small seaport it was very difficult to reach the rest of Scotland. The roads were poor. Though Callander was only fifty miles distant as the crow flew it was half as much again by the shortest road route. Moreover a horse-drawn coach could not carry many passengers. The valley-route to Callander was the most direct way towards Perth, Dundee, Stirling and Edinburgh. As for Glasgow, one had the choice of going there by road or by water. The road-route went eastwards as far as Dalmally and continued by way of Inveraray, the head of Loch Fyne, the Rest-and-be-Thankful Pass, Arrochar, Gareloch-head and Helensburgh, making a total of about a hundred miles, with many steep pitches. Passengers might use such a route, but for merchandise in bulk it was out of the question. The route by water was along the coast south-westwards to the entry to the Crinan Canal, then along the latter with its many locks as far as Ardrishaig; then round the southern tip of the island of Bute, then up the Clyde estuary. The journey was well over a hundred miles and took more than one day to accomplish. Oban and the islands in its vicinity were more isolated from the more populous parts of Scotland in the mid-nineteenth century than, say, Orkney and Shetland are now. Even the most basic single line railway would be an inestimable boon. So the pressure for a rail link came principally from Oban, and at long last it was gained.

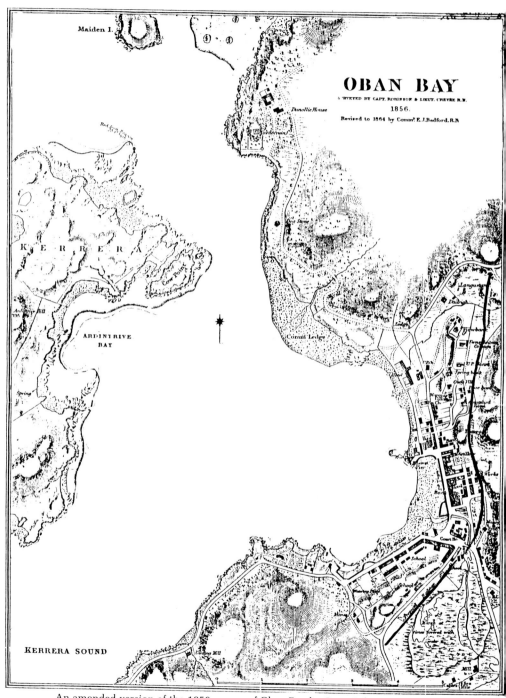

An amended version of the 1856 survey of Oban Bay by Capt. Robinson showing the route of the proposed railway.

Based on the map, courtesy of the Scottish Record Office

Chapter Two
Preliminaries to Construction

The growing interest felt in and around Oban during the early 1860s in a rail link that would facilitate access to and from the populous central belt of Scotland issued in the formation of a committee of twenty-four residents in the Oban area. Two legal gentlemen, Henry Inglis of Edinburgh and James Keydon of Glasgow were commissioned to contact other railway companies and ascertain whether any of them might be interested in supporting such a venture and, if so, would be willing to contribute towards it by taking shares. These promoters knew very well that they could never command sufficient funds to build the line without outside help, let alone run it when it had been built. The thing to do was to find a sympathetic partner which would see in such a line a prospect for added profit for itself and would be ready to provide the locomotives, rolling stock and operating necessities as well as the necessary paid labour.

Callander seemed the most likely place from which such a railway should be built. This large village, the gateway to the romantic scenery of the Trossachs and Loch Katrine, had already been reached from the east by the Dunblane, Doune and Callander Railway, which had first been promoted by local residents in Callander as early as 1846 and had been given Parliamentary sanction, but had then lapsed through lack of money before being revived a few years later. It was finished in 1858. At its eastern end it joined the Scottish Central, which shortly afterwards took it over. The latter railway was based on Perth, linked that city with Dundee and Stirling and extended south of the last-named town to reach the Caledonian, thus providing a link with Carlisle and the South, and had running powers into Edinburgh and Glasgow. It was therefore an important company, and one of those to which Messrs Inglis and Keydon turned for support.

However, there was another option worth consideration. When possible routes eastward from Oban were under review the lie of the land more or less dictated that the first forty miles or so should follow the southern shore of Loch Etive, reach Loch Awe along the Pass of Brander, skirt its broad northern end, follow the valleys of the Orchy and Lochy through Dalmally to the watershed between eastern and western Scotland near Tyndrum and then aim south-east to the village of Crianlarich. Beyond here there were two possible routes. Though it was only thirty more miles to Callander the natural route of the Dochart valley could only be used for six miles or so, after which it would be necessary to climb along the hillside to reach the gap leading to Glen Ogle, more than 900 ft above sea level. There would then have to be a steep descent past Lochearnhead to the entrance to the Braes of Balquhidder, a few level miles beside Loch Lubnaig, and finally a piercing of the defile beside the Falls of Leny to reach Callander. On the other hand, if the line from Crianlarich onwards were instead to strike south-westward down the Falloch valley to Ardlui, skirt the eastern side of Loch Lomond, surmount the low pass east of Invernaid and then follow the valley of the Water of Chon past Lochs Chon and Ard to Aberfoyle, it would then approach the Forth and Clyde Junction and Blane valley railways and so be able to reach Glasgow. This route to the latter city would be shorter than by way of Callander and Stirling, though somewhat further to Edinburgh, and Glasgow was, then as now, a much larger city than the capital.

Accordingly Messrs Inglis and Keydon contacted not only the Scottish Central but the Forth and Clyde Junction and Blane Valley railways as well, and for good measure included in their enquiries the Caledonian, North British and Edinburgh and Glasgow railways, none of which would come directly into contact with the proposed line from Oban by either route, but all of which might be interested in promoting it in case it brought them traffic.

All six companies reacted favourably and three expressed a readiness to buy shares. The Forth and Clyde and the Blane Valley, making a joint response, urged that the Loch Lomond route be adopted, and offered between them to contribute £70,000. The Scottish Central went a great deal better, expressing itself willing to put £200,000 into a line routed by way of Callander, provided that the remainder of the money needed for construction were raised in the line's locality. The promoters met again on 8th July, 1864, and heard what Inglis and Keydon had to tell them. At a second meeting two-and-a-half weeks later they came to a decision. Although the supporters of the Loch Lomond-side route had pressed their proposal strongly, and it certainly had its merits, the difference between an offer of £70,000 and one nearly three times as great was the deciding factor. The Scottish Central Railway's proposal was accepted.

Then began a period of haggling over the details of the agreement by which the latter line should work the new line after it had been made. There was some dragging of feet on the Scottish Central's part, and some concern that the balance of the money, estimated at £400,000 might not after all be raised locally. It was not anxious to find itself part-owner of a pig in a poke. It made certain conditions about the quality of the work to be done. Rails were to weigh not less than 75 lb. to the yard and were to be in lengths of 24 ft; sleepers were to be spaced 3 ft apart; none of the bridges was to be made of timber. If they were to supply locomotives, coaches, wagons and all other necessary appurtenances to the working of the line, they claimed the right to appoint and dismiss staff, and to receive half the line's gross revenue.

Eventually agreement was reached and a Bill was drawn up for approval by Parliament. On 7th November, 1864 this was published. It began impressively:

NOTICE IS HEREBY GIVEN, that it is intended to apply to Parliament in the next Session for leave to bring in a Bill for making and maintaining the following Railway and Tramway, or one of them, or part thereof, with all proper Stations, Approaches and other Works and Conveniences connected therewith, viz.:–

First, a Railway commencing at or near a point about two furlongs southwestwards from the School-house in the town of Oban, called the Oban Industrial School, and terminating by a Junction with the Dunblane, Doune and Callander Railway at or near a point about one and a half furlongs eastward from the Booking Office attached to the Callander Station of the said Dunblane, Doune and Callander Railway.

Secondly, a Tramway commencing by a Junction with the proposed Raiway above described, at or near a point about one furlong south-westward from the said School-house, and terminating on the Pier on the East side of the Harbour of the said town of Oban at or near a point about two chains eastward from the south-westward end of the said Pier.

Which Railway and Tramway and Works, and the lands, houses and other herit-ages which may be taken for the purposes thereof will be and are situate in, and will pass from, through or into the following places, or some of them – that is to say, the town of Oban, the united parishes of Kilmore and Kilbride, the united parishes of Ardchattan and Muckairn and the united parishes of Glenorchy and Inishail, all in the County of Argyle, and the parishes of Killin, Balquhidder and Callander, all in the County of Perth.

AND NOTICE IS ALSO GIVEN, that duplicate Plans and Sections, describing the lines, situation and levels of the said intended Railway and Tramway, and the lands, houses and other heritages through which the same are intended to be made, and within the limits of deviation as defined on the said Plans, and which may be required to be taken for the purposes of the said Works, together with a Book of Reference to such Plans, containing the names of the owners, or reputed owners, lessees or reputed lessees, and occupiers of such lands, houses and other heritages respectively, and a Published Map showing thereon the general course and direction of the said proposed Railway and Tramway, and also a copy of this notice, as it will be published in the *Edinburgh Gazette*, will be deposited for public inspection on or before the 30th day of the present month of November, in the Office, at Inverary, of the principal Sheriff-Clerk of the County of Argyle, and in the Offices, at Dunblane and Perth respectively, of the principal Sheriff-Clerk of the County of Perth; and that a copy of so much of the said Plans, Sections and Book of References as relates to each of the said parishes, with a copy of this Notice as aforesaid, will, on or before the said 30th day of the present month of November be deposited for public inspection with the Schoolmaster, if any, and if there be no Schoolmaster, with the Session Clerk of each of the said parishes, at the place of abode of such Schoolmaster or Session Clerk.

The Bill, continuing in similar legal language, provided where the line would run, stated that powers would be applied for to alter if necessary exis-ting highways, natural features and man-made "conveniences," that the company would seek powers to raise all necessary money to construct the line and to levy tolls and charges for using it, and that an agreement would be made with the Scottish Central so that the latter should work the railway with its own engines and rolling stock, and staff it with its own clerks, of-ficers and servants. The last of the paragraphs quoted above indicates the traditional status of the dominie in Scotland, who was regarded as more important than the local lay representative of the Kirk.

In January 1865 Parliamentary approval was given, and six months later the Bill became an Act. Now the work of construction could begin. But in fact it did not begin. No sooner did the Act become law than, the very next day, the Scottish Central Railway ceased to exist, since the Caledonian Railway took it over, with all its obligations and commitments, and it became a part of the Caledonian system. In the Callander and Oban line, to the Board of which it was now entitled to nominate a majority of the Directors, the Caledonian found itself responsible for a system which promised to be a liability rather than an asset. Nevertheless, it had to make the best of it – and was later to be glad it had done so.

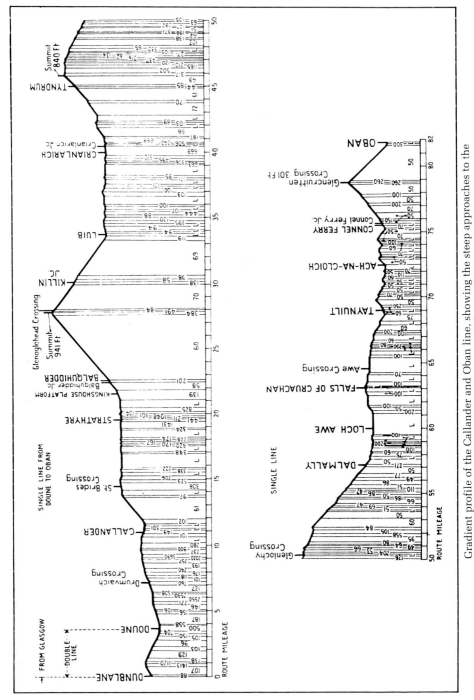

Gradient profile of the Callander and Oban line, showing the steep approaches to the three summits at Glenoglehead, Tyndrum and Glencruitten.

Chapter Three
Getting off to a Slow Start

The association of the Scottish Central with the Callander and Oban Railway would have been a marriage of convenience for both parties, each seeing in the other a source of increased revenue once the latter actually became a going concern. To the Caledonian the new venture seemed at first an unwanted and unattractive addition to a harem of newly-acquired brides each of which, from a shareholder's point of view, was potentially more fruitful. However, the Caledonian did have the right to refuse to work any trains on the C & O unless at least twenty miles had been constructed. Whether even that amount could be achieved was a doubtful question. The £400,000 which it had been undertaken to raise locally was not yet in the kitty. To the pessimistic Caledonian Directors it seemed unlikely that anything approaching that figure could ever be raised. The Marquess of Breadalbane and the Duke of Argyll had both promised support, but after that it was a matter of scraping the barrel, and the first call for subscribers to put their money where their mouths had been yielded only a seventh of the amount required. So, for over a year, nothing was done.

At this juncture the Callander and Oban was so fortunate as to secure the service, as their Secretary, of a rather remarkable man, notable not so much for his intellectual abilities (though these were not lacking) as for a bulldog-like persistence in seeking the Company's advantage. Like Matthew Arnold's Scholar Gypsy, he had one aim, one business, one desire: to promote the interest of the company to which he had linked his own fortunes. He was at first only a salaried servant earning £250 a year, out of which he had to pay the wages of a clerk. But he was also permitted to supplement his income by acting as Secretary to the Glasgow Shale Oil Company and conducting that firm's business from the Callander and Oban's Glasgow office in Dundas Street, paying the Company seven guineas a year for the concession.

John Anderson, when he was appointed, was still a comparatively young man, who had held the post of assistant general manager to the Edinburgh and Glasgow Railway until the North British swallowed it up. His new post must have seemed something of a come-down, but he determined to make the most of it. He remained Secretary for over forty years and in a manner of speaking *was* the company. Others might sit on the Board or have a financial stake; he was the one who conducted its operations day by day, and because of his close knowledge of it soon became indispensable. In the Scottish Record Office's archives in Edinburgh fourteen letter-books contain copies of his voluminous correspondence. His first duty after being appointed was above all to secure money so that the line could be built. He sent out letters to all and sundry, high and low, who had promised support, varying his approach according to the importance of the recipient. He requested, urged, cajoled or implored as the case suggested, using standard forms of letter, each for a different category of people. He also went out paying visits to canvass for support, going hat in hand to shops and small businesses in Oban and elsewhere. He endeavoured to woo from their existing allegiances those who had promised to support other railways, denigrating their prospects and painting those of the Callander and Oban in rosy colours. In other words, he was up to all the tricks of the trade. The company could have had no more diligent and astute servant.

A Mr Blyth (the records give no initials) who had been an engineer on the Scottish Central and Sir Donald Campbell were chosen as Joint Engineers of the line, to make the first surveys; the former had responsibility for the section from Callander to Dalmally, the latter for the line beyond. In August 1865, when he had received no word about getting started, Blyth wrote to Anderson to press that the survey should be begun, since the coming of winter would hamper operations. Anderson replied explaining about the shortage of money, so Blyth suggested that if the work could not be done in its entirety, at least the section nearest to Callander should be set in hand. He suggested taking a survey as far as the head of Glen Ogle, some 17½ miles from Callander. Anderson managed to get the Board's agreement to this, which was somewhat surprising, since even if that length of track were laid down and could be used for traffic the Caledonian would still be entitled to refuse to work it, since it did not amount to 20 miles. However, the latter's representatives on the Board made no difficulties, and Blyth was told he could begin his surveying.

It was now necessary to find a contractor who would undertake the construction along the route indicated in the survey. Tenders were invited; ten were submitted; the Board accepted the lowest, that of John Mackay, of £124,218, on 31st July, 1866. It was stipulated that the work had to be completed between 1st May and 1st July, 1869. The first sod was turned on 29th October and the influx of navvies began. Contrary to expectation they were well-behaved and no fights or riots are recorded. One police constable was employed to patrol the line as it extended. Anderson vetoed a suggestion that there should be two; costs had to be pared to a minimum and so long as no trouble was reported a mere token assertion of the majesty of the law was thought enough.

There were some awkward moments during the building of the line. Landowners were quick to claim immediate compensation when digging began in their properties, or even when the surveyors arrived with their theodolites. Demands were made on the occasion of this or that inconvenience. Sir Malcolm MacGregor of Edinchip pressed for the line to be carried under his estate in a tunnel, which would have cost an extra £9,000, but Parliament disallowed such unnecessary extravagance. At the same time the terms of the Act insisted that all work had to be confined within the specified boundaries on either side of the centre line of the route; no spoil was to be shovelled to right or left and no side cuttings made. This restriction involved a good deal of cartage of soil and stones back along the line.

Meanwhile the money was coming in all too slowly, and Anderson was busy trying to raise it and conserve what was already there. This meant, among other things, postponing compensation payments as long as possible. Sir Malcolm MacGregor was entitled to £2500 as soon as ground was broken on his land, so Anderson asked Mackay to delay doing this as long as he could and to work on either side of Edinchip estate without actually penetrating its boundaries until the last moment. This was awkward for the contractor; it meant that the rails which had been laid down, as they followed the embanking and excavating, could not be used for bringing up or taking away materials beyond the southern boundary of Edinchip, and road wagons had to do the work beyond.

In the summer of 1867 the permanent way began to be laid down. The rails were of assorted lengths; most were 24 ft long but a number were shorter, some being only of 18 ft. In August of that year the sacred soil of Edinchip estate was at last invaded, the workmen being given strict injunctions not to do the slightest damage outside the stated boundaries. One of Sir Malcolm's factors was always present to see that orders were obeyed. All seemed to be going well, when the Caledonian Railway suddenly threw a spanner in the works, saying that construction was to be suspended for the winter. As the Caledonian had a majority of the Directors on the Board they were in a strong position. Anderson tried to reason with them. To stop work, he pointed out, would look bad and make it even more difficult for him to get money subscribed. If the contractor were forced to withdrawn his men and plant he would have to be compensated. The men themselves did more work during the winter that during the summer, in proportion to the time they were employed. The Caledonian, however, was insistent. Either work stopped for the winter or the contractor would have to agree to accept a token payment while it went on. Mackay reluctantly agreed to this and the work continued. In March of the following year Blyth reported that, though the weather had been stormy, no damage from rain or flood had been done to the works, which were now well advanced towards completion. "We have studied throughout," he wrote, "to make the works substantial yet with a due regard for economy. The line, while passing through a difficult country, will be made in all respects secure and will undoubtedly be the most beautiful in Scotland."

The Caledonian Directors on the Board were unimpressed, and pressure grew for the curtailment of the line. Oban seemed impossibly far away; money was coming in slowly in spite of all Anderson's efforts; the work on the line itself slowed down as the difficult part along the west side of Glen Ogle was reached. By the end of 1868 the first stage to Glenoglehead was still not finished. The non-Caledonian members of the Board eventually shrugged their shoulders and agreed to limit their ambitions. A Callander and Oban (Abandonment) Bill was framed, which sought to limit the Company's obligation to continuing the line as far as the County March between Perthshire and Argyllshire, just west of Tyndrum. The authorized capital was reduced to £243,000 and the Caledonian's contribution to £162,000. Extra time was to be allowed for completing the line to Tyndrum. It was all very disheartening to the promoters, who began to realize they had bitten off more than they could chew. The Caledonian had some difficulty in persuading their shareholders that this compromise was in their best interests, but they were eventually brought to accept that the truncated line would not be merely a white elephant. If it reached Tyndrum it could connect with traffic by road from west and north.

By the summer of 1868 the permanent way had been placed in position as far as the site of the later Balquhidder Junction and a coal depot was set up there. Coal traffic now began from the Scottish coalfields by way of Dunblane, the empty trucks returning with timber. The line could now make a contribution towards paying for itself, and the new facility was much appreciated locally. It is probable that a certain amount of clandestine passenger travel also took place, in the contractors' vehicles, or even on their locomotive. Anderson turned a blind eye to this; it was important not to offend the contractor while he was still constructing the line, and if he made a little on the side moving people as well as goods, that was neither here nor there.

At long last, in the spring of 1870, the first seventeen and a half miles were completed, and a station named Killin was opened at the top of the Pass at Glenoglehead, just beyond the small Loch Larig Eala. From here to Killin it is a full four miles, and any use of the station by the villagers was limited by the need to make a long and tiring journey on foot or in a conveyance before the railhead could be reached. At the other end of the line a new station was built just behind the main hotel, the Dreadnought Inn, at Callander; from here the line extended eastward to link up with the existing branch from Dunblane. Going westward from Callander the first station was at Strathyre, a small village about a mile beyond the head of Loch Lubnaig; another station two miles farther on, the later Balquhidder Junction, was called Lochearnhead, though the village of that name was another two miles away. It would not have been possible to give the latter a convenient station any closer, since immediately beyond the more distant one the line begins to rise on a steep gradient along the hillside, bearing round Edinchip house and climbing steadily, so that at the nearest point to Lochearnhead village it is already 400 ft above the latter.

The station at Callander was a two-platform affair, not as large as the one that later replaced it. Strathyre, Lochearnhead and Killin each had a single platform, and at the last-named plenty of siding-space was provided, as well as a turntable and an engine shed. All the stations were timber-built. The line was signalled to work on a staff-and-token system, for under £500. Everything was done as cheaply as possible; there was no money for luxuries or frills. Anderson himself shopped around to get cheap fire-grates and wooden benches for the stations.

As to locomotives and rolling stock, this was a matter for the Caledonian, and Anderson consulted with Benjamin Conner, the latter's locomotive superintendent, since some of the line's structures limited their dimensions – in particular the bridges which crossed the river in the Pass of Leny. The Caledonian offered to run four trains a day in each direction, but Anderson thought this would be too many and suggested two; in the end they compromised on three. Having found when they were to run, Anderson arranged with coach firms at Crieff and Aberfeldy so that connections could be provided for the trains; clearly not much traffic could be expected at Killin Station unless vehicles plied to and from it.

Next came the business of getting Board of Trade approval. An inspector, Captain Tyler, was sent, and went over the whole line thoroughly in company with Anderson, Blyth and one of the company's Directors. The latter did their best to put Tyler in a favourable mood; he was lodged at

Edinchip rather than at an hotel. However, he left without expressing an opinion. Later, when Anderson was beginning to get worked up about whether the line would be approved after all, Tyler returned to make a further check and then dropped a broad hint that it would be all right to advertise the opening for the 1st June.

And so it was. At a quarter past seven in the morning on 1st June, 1870 the first train left Killin for Callander with over a hundred passengers, some of whom had walked up from Killin during the small hours. At eleven o'clock a special train set out from Callander for Killin, carrying local persons of importance and invited guests. At Strathyre and Lochearnhead the inhabitants turned out in numbers to meet and cheer the train. The highlight came as it began to climb the gradient beyond Lochearnhead, providing a magnificent view down the Earn valley and the whole length of the Loch from its exalted elevation on the hillside. At Killin there was a long wait before the return journey; some who had come down by the earlier train now returned to Killin village on foot or by coach; others wandered over the mountainside or walked down the road to pick the train up at Lochearnhead as it travelled back. Anderson afterwards reckoned that it had been a very successful opening. Some of the usual accompaniments on an occasion of this sort, it is true, were missing. There was no concluding beanfeast at the Dreadnought Hotel. There were no congratulatory speeches. The latter would in any case have been premature; Oban had not yet been reached. Celebrations would also have been expensive, and the Company now had less than £25,000 in hand towards the extension to Tyndrum. However, it now had a source of receipts to set against further expenditure.

A special train about to leave Stirling station with opening-day guests. The locomotive is ex-Scottish Central 2–2–2 No. 301 and ran as far as Callander.
Courtesy, David and Charles

Opening-day banquet at Oban Station. Note that the ladies were confined to the waiting room in the background.   *Courtesy, David and Charles*

John Anderson (*centre*) and official inspection party at Taynuilt in 1880.
                                                 Courtesy, David and Charles

Chapter Four
Advancing into Argyll

It was a fair comment on the first instalment of the Callander and Oban Railway that it went nowhere in particular, and many made it. However, during the first summer of its existence as a going concern it had a certain novelty value, and the Caledonian were ready enough to take advantage of this and run special Saturday excursions along it. By making an early start in Glasgow one might spend as long as six hours contemplating the gloomy glories of the head of Glen Ogle – or, more pleasantly, some five hours in Killin itself, since a coach link was arranged from that village. In this way began the sequence of visitors that has never since ended (though now they mostly come by car or motor-coach), of day tourists coming to admire the cascade of the Dochart from the parapet of the stone bridge near the old burial ground of the MacNabs, and to wander over the rocks. In 1870 this excursion cost 4s. 6d. return from Glasgow to the terminal platform at the head of Glen Ogle, from which for a further 1s. 6d. return they could be taken down to Killin itself.

It was also now possible to make a connection with a horse-drawn coach service going to or returning from Oban and Ballachulish, and this journey could be made in one day if one left Glasgow early enough. The single fare for the additional coach journey was 11s. for an inside seat and 17s. for an outside one. The people of Killin disliked this intrusion of a Ballachulish entrepreneur, however, into business that should have been theirs, and refused to stable the horses overnight, so Anderson had a wooden shed built near the station where they could be accommodated.

The ordinary weekday train service during this first summer was as follows:

Callander, dep.:	9.35 am	11.10 am	6.00 pm
Killin, arr.:	11.00 am	12.10 pm	7.00 pm
and in the opposite direction:			
Killin, dep.:	7.15 am	2.40 pm	6.20 pm
Callander, arr.:	8.15 am	4.00 pm	7.30 pm

All trains in either direction halted at Strathyre and Lochearnhead. It is not clear why two of the trains took so much longer than the even hour for the journey, which latter only involved a speed of 17½ miles an hour. Possibly it had to do with the need to stop and attach or detach wagons; it was certainly not so that one train could pass another, as an inspection of the timetable shows. By the end of the summer the service had been reduced to two trains each way daily.

The first six months' receipts amounted to a little over £2500, which Anderson regarded with satisfaction. He felt that the special excursion trains had been well worth while, and wished them to continue throughout the year on Saturdays, but the Caledonian did not share his expectations and would not oblige. Anderson had a hand in writing the advertising copy for the excursions, and described them as an opportunity for people to "visit the Khyber Pass of Scotland," which was not really a happy likeness, possibly suggesting that local tribesmen would take pot shots at intruders from their ancient matchlocks. No doubt he was thinking in terms of wild and savage scenery, but Glen Ogle is not a very dreadful sight – much less awe-inspiring than Glencoe or the Lairig Ghru. Fishermen as well as scenery-worshippers were also catered for. An angler could exercise his right to stop the train near a lochside farm two miles short of Strathyre and spend the day on Loch Lubnaig, plying his rod from a hired boat.

Meanwhile the extension of the Callander and Oban's existing line was being taken in hand. Parliamentary sanction existed for its construction as far as Tyndrum, and tenders were called for. Easton Gibb of Cardiff submitted the lowest tender – £69,261 – and this was accepted. A little later the contractor discovered an arithmetical error in his calculations, which annoyed the Callander and Oban's Directors very much, though it only amounted to £100. The work went ahead, but not to the Board's satisfaction; minutes of their meetings repeatedly express dissatisfaction at the slow rate of progress. The terrain was not as difficult as that which had faced Mackay when he built the first stage, but the contractor underestimated how much the work would cost, and, one assumes, slowed down to save expenses. In September 1872 the Board consulted Blyth about the possibility of withholding payment to Easton Gibb as a disciplinary measure. However, this was not done, and the line was eventually finished in August 1873. Stations were built at Luib, Crianlarich and Tyndrum, and at the latter place extensive sidings were laid out for the reception of coaches and wagons. The engine shed at Killin was also dismantled and re-erected at Tyndrum. To get the line so far it had been necessary to overdraw at the bank to the extent of £2500. However, the Company was now half way towards its ultimate goal, and the coaches which had formerly met the trains at Killin now did so at the new railhead, which was right on the edge of Perthshire and almost on the watershed between eastern and western Scotland.

The summer excursions that John Anderson was so anxious to promote could now be extended. The village of Crianlarich is only nine miles from the northern end of Loch Lomond; another ten miles further on was Arrochar at the head of Loch Long. Clyde steamers connected Arrochar with Glasgow, and Loch Lomond also had a steamer service. Circular tours were arranged in which the railway was used as far as Crianlarich; coaches met the trains there and took tourists on to connect with the Loch Lomond and Loch Long steamers. A more extended tour could be had by travelling from Glasgow on a MacBrayne steamer to Ardrishaig on Loch Fyne, where a coach could be boarded which followed the western shore of that loch to Inveraray, continued along Glen Aray to Dalmally and then went on to Tyndrum to connect with the train again. More venturesomely and perhaps more riskily Anderson tried to promote mountain-climbing. The great hill of Ben More looms above Crianlarich to a height less than 600 ft lower than that of Ben Nevis itself, and in summer presents no problems for those who are properly shod. Anderson asked the hotel-keeper at Crianlarich to provide guides to conduct excursionists to the summit on the arrival of the first train from Callander. Although the path up the mountain presents no special difficulties, it is long and strenuous, and would have been a tough assignment for anyone not experienced in mountain walking, especially if he were not wearing suitable boots.

The basic winter train service from Callander to Tyndrum took from two hours to two hours and twenty minutes, and the trains were a mere two coaches, some having vans or wagons attached as well. They did not run at times most convenient to their users, for the Caledonian insisted on a time-table which suited them, fitting in with their own rostering of engines and rolling stock. There was a nine hours' gap between the morning departure from Callander at 9.40 am and the evening one; in the opposite direction the first train left Tyndrum at the ridiculous time of 5.30 am; the next and last was at two in the afternoon. Anderson had a good deal of correspondence with the Caledonian about this and other aspects of the train services. He believed that his company was being charged too much for the hire of the locomotives and submitted figures purporting to prove it. He complained bitterly that trains from the south arrived frequently so late at Callander. The Caledonian eventually managed to show that it was not their fault, but that the North British were handing over their trains to them even later and that fast running on Caldeonian metals recouped some of the lost time.

Despite having provided extensive sidings at Tyndrum, the Callander and Oban still meant to take their line further west. The Abandonment Act which had been passed in 1870 was followed by another request to Parliament, to extend the line to Oban as originally intended. As long as the railway led through poor country, nowhere touching any sizeable popu-lation centre, its receipts could never increase sufficiently to pay all the company's expenses. Only if it reached Oban could a source of sufficient income be gained. Anderson returned to the task of canvassing for further subscriptions, and tenders were sought for an extension to Dalmally, which was twelve miles beyond Tyndrum and well into Argyllshire. John Mackay, who had built the first stage of the line, was given the contract in March 1875. Compared with the two previous stages he had a comparatively easy task, which was reflected in his low tender of £36,408. The first half of the line's course, through a comparatively level and bare valley, presented no special difficulties. After that it was necessary to excavate on the slopes below Ben Lui to bring the line down to Dalmally at an altitude of 250 ft above the sea, and one large bridge was required on this section, over the Eas a'Ghallt burn, whose eventual completion was celebrated on the spot by dancing, potations of whisky and the playing of bagpipes. Dalmally was reached on 1st May, 1877 and a handsome stone station was built there.

Once more John Anderson could employ himself organizing circular tours in conjunction with coach and steamer operators. The rail timetable that summer showed faster running than before. Trains left Dalmally for Callander taking just two hours for the forty-six miles' journey, at a quarter to six in the morning (another example of the Caledonian's cussedness), at half past one, and again at five pm; similar times were made returning from Callander at 9.20 am, 11.7 am and 6.10 pm. From Oban to Glasgow it now took eight and a half hours, by means of coaches connecting with the 1.30 and 5 pm trains at Dalmally. Alternatively one might leave Oban at 7 pm, put up for the night at Dalmally, make an early start from there and reach Glasgow at 9.30 the next morning; a similar combination of evening train and morning coach was available in the opposite direction. Average speeds on the rail section, of 22½ mph between Callander and Dalmally, contrasted with a mere 7 mph on the road section, and demonstrated the superiority of the railway beyond all question.

Callander Station seen here in pre-grouping days, looking east from the end of the down platform. Note the ornate footbridge and clock tower.

L.G.R.P. Collection, courtesy David and Charles

The forecourt of Callander Station, photographed during the 'thirties, with adverts for steamboats on Loch Katrine and Trossachs Tours.

L.G.R.P. Collection, courtesy David and Charles

Chapter Five
The Project Accomplished

A year after Dalmally had been reached the construction of the final 24 miles of the line was taken in hand. There had to be an interval in which further funds could be accumulated, and John Anderson was kept busy trying to raise them. He had a stroke of luck. Impressed, perhaps, by the possibilities of a completed railway, and perhaps thinking in terms of through traffic from Euston to Oban (though it was still to be some time before that journey could be made without changing carriages), the Board of the London and North Western Railway decided to subscribe a substantial amount and purchased £50,000 worth of preference shares. This seems to have been a demonstration of faith in the line's eventual success as a business venture, and not an attempt to control its destinies. Although the LNWR was told that it might now nominate a Director to the Callander and Oban Board, it was not one of its own men that was chosen. What actually happened was that the Marquess of Breadalbane, who was already on the Board, representing the C & O, resigned and was immediately re-elected as the LNW's representative.

There was, therefore, going to be no money problem during the final stage, which was as well, since engineering difficulties cropped up of a kind not hitherto met. First there was a wide river valley to be crossed, that of the Orchy just before this stream entered Loch Awe, and this required a seven-span girder bridge. Then came a tricky section in which the railway had to follow the line of the coach road along the northern shore of Loch Awe, where the slopes of the many-peaked Ben Cruachan came steeply down to the water's edge. For much of this section it was necessary to blast a path through solid granite in order to make a shelf along which to lay the line. Once past Cruachan, and having negotiated the narrow defile of the Pass of Brander, the route had to swing round to the left to cross the deep channel of the River Awe just before it drained into Loch Etive, and a high girder bridge was needed to span it. Then, after a fairly easy stretch to the village of Taynuilt, the southern shore of Loch Etive was reached, and here, to cut excavation to a minimum, the line needed to follow the contours of the land and so had to be rather sinuous. Lastly came a six-mile up-and-down gable, steeply graded, to the head of Glen Cruitten and down that valley's southern side, Oban being approached as it were from the rear since the track had to make a great loop in order to reach sea level without steepening to more than 1 in 50.

A new surveyor was chosen for the final section, John Strain of Glasgow, who was later appointed as Engineer for the whole line. Contractors were selected to construct the line in two almost equal lengths simultaneously, Messrs W. and T. Adams for the Dalmally-Taynuilt section, and Ireland and Company of Montrose for the final stretch. It was therefore possible to finish the whole length of 24 miles in two years. Stations were established near the Loch Awe Hotel (beside which a pier was built for steamers plying on the Loch), and at Taynuilt and Connel Ferry.

The approach to Oban itself brought problems of a different kind. Opinion was divided within the town about the course the line ought to take. Everyone was glad of the advantages the railway would bring, but there were also fears that civic amenities might be spoiled. The Obanians were proud of their bay and the prospect from it, towards the rolling humpy hills of the island of Kerrera and, beyond that, to the mountains of Mull. The town's main street curved round the bay from south to north towards a pier on the northern end, to which the boats from the islands came. The railway station was to be placed south of the bay – exactly where had not been settled – and as the line approached the terminus a branch tramway was to lead off to the left, which according to the terms of the Act of Parliament would link the railway with the existing pier. The only way in which this could be done was by making an embankment which paralleled the main street, coming between it and the sea. When the Bill had been first published there had been concern that the tramway should not make an unsightly passage beside the town's most attractive street, and it had been opposed. But the most the objecting townsfolk could then achieve was a stipulation that such a tramway should not encroach on the streets nor be worked by locomotives or a stationary engine with ropes. Presumably horses would have to be employed. But an embankment there had to be or the railway would not be able to serve the pier at all.

For some time feeling ran high in Oban as the toiling navvies brought the railway nearer. Pro- and anti-embankment factions argued it out in the local newspapers. The first were prepared to welcome both railway and tramway, warts and all, because of the economic blessings it would bring. The second thought only in terms of eyesores and the destruction of amenities. What was the use, the objectors asked, of making access easier to visitors if the charms of the place they were visiting were thus disfigured? They would come once, dislike what they saw and never return. On the other side it was urged that contact with the steamers, for transhipment of passengers and goods, was absolutely necessary.

Then the Company cut the Gordian knot by determining to build a new pier on the south side of the bay, on land that had been recently reclaimed. At once new objections were raised. This, too, would constitute an eyesore. Moreover, some people's pockets were threatened. John MacCaig, a wealthy townsman, who actually owned the old pier, objected most strongly. MacCraig was a rather eccentric character who later displayed his civic feeling by building what was supposed to be a replica of the Colosseum in Rome above the town on the top of an eminence. The structure was never finished and remains to the present day as a "folly", unique of its kind, which has never served any useful purpose whatever. MacCaig certainly had money to throw away, but the threat of the new pier attracting boats away from the older one alarmed him, and he poured scorn on the railway's proposals. However the latter had its way and did build the new pier and the tramway to it, though it had to pay heavily for the land on which it was built. The owner, one of its own Directors, asked £20,000; the company offered under £3000; the dispute went to arbitration and in the end they compromised on nearly £5400.

Meanwhile the workings were drawing nearer and the navvies were beginning to spend their wages within the town. This was excellent so long as they caused no trouble and there were no drunken riots in the streets. Among the objects on which the workmens' money was expended was the produce of the local distillery, which suited the distillers very well but the more sober among the townsfolk feared for the consequences. Temperance advocates established refreshment booths at the places where the men worked, staffed by volunteers, where the meretricious attractions of alcohol were countered by the provision of cheap tea, coffee and soft drinks. The enthusiasm of these missionaries even brought about some temporary conversions; a number of navvies signed the pledge and deposited the cash so saved in savings' banks.

By the spring of 1880 the pace of construction quickened so that the work could be completed by midsummer. A splendid terminal station arose on the south side of the bay, made of wood and glass, as were nearly all the other C&O stations, but crowned by an impressive clock tower with a spire. It was on its concourse that the great celebratory dinner was held, on 30th June, 1880, the proudest day in John Anderson's life. The whole town of Oban put aside its disagreements and gave itself up to a day of rejoicing and junketing. The usual Queen's Birthday holiday was transferred to the commemoration of this more important event. The interior of the new station was decorated with a flower display organized by Mrs John Anderson. The tables set on the concourse were spread by the management of the Glasgow and South Western Railway's St Enoch Hotel. Regrettably the weather was not kind for the occasion; rain fell heavily and the hills were shrouded in mist. However, the damp did not reach within the station's glazed roof, where the only moisture was that which went down the diners' throats.

Local dignitaries came in procession along the streets, presumably under umbrellas. A special steamer arrived, from Holyhead of all places, bringing representatives of the London and North Western Railway. Eventually a special train carrying further guests arrived from the east behind two locomotives. Cheers and rousing music from local bands greeted it, and fog detonators added cacophony to harmony as the locomotive's wheels ran over them — the railway equivalent of a salute of guns. Eventually everyone settled down to eat and drink. After that there were speeches, some sensible, some fatuous, all in good humour. Among the sensible ones was John Anderson's in which he recounted the vicissitudes the line had gone through before final victory, and he did not spare to mention "lukewarm friends and open foes," some of whom were probably listening to him. It was his great day, not only regarding his pride but also his pocket, for his salary was now raised to £700 a year and he was made traffic manager as well as Secretary. He moved house to Oban and remained there till he retired in 1907.

Reaching Oban at last had an immediate effect on the line's fortunes. The revenue for the first six months from the end of June 1880 was, at just over £9500, three-and-a-half times greater than it had been in the same period the previous year. The distance run by the trains during that time was a little over twice as much as before; the line was therefore being used more profitably as well as more intensively. During the summer months as many as five passenger trains traversed the whole distance between Callander and Oban in both directions daily, though this was somewhat reduced, and the trains themselves shortened, during the winter. There were also, of course, many special excursion trains. The fastest of the regular ones, the up evening train from Oban, took only two hours and forty-three minutes to Callander, at an average speed of 26½ mph, stopping at all stations; to the end of the steam period no timing was very much better than that. In the reverse direction the slowest train, the 11.48 pm from Callander, which carried the mails and had to make lengthy stops, took its time and did not get to Oban till 4.35 am – nearly five hours. But a horse-drawn coach, allowing for stops, changing of horses and taking refreshments, would probably have taken twelve hours.

Steamer services using Oban, under John Anderson's prodding finger, began to alter their schedules so as to connect with convenient trains. Boats plied to Fort William, Tobermory on Mull, and places in between. It became possible for islanders to reach Edinburgh or Glasgow in the same day. Day excursions were also organized by coach or steamer to places as far afield as Glen Etive and the Pass of Melfort, and were highly popular. The line was less used for freight traffic since a good steamer service at low rates already existed to Glasgow, and speed did not matter as much as cheapness in regard to goods in bulk. The Callander and Oban was predominantly a passenger railway, and in particular a summer tourist railway; it made its profits between June and September, when the visitors came in their thousands. Over what is now left of the line (1987) this is still the case.

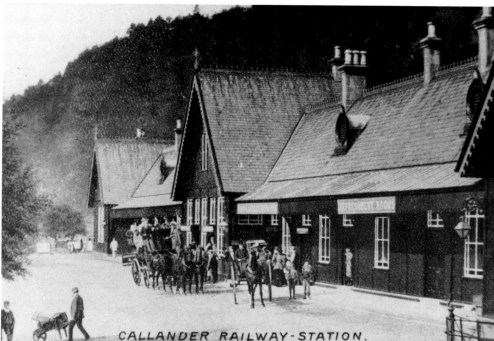

CALLANDER RAILWAY-STATION.

An early view of Callander Station forecourt with the coach and four ready to convey passengers to their destinations, c.1895.   *H.M.R.S. Collection*

Chapter Six
The Route Described

In this chapter the past tense is used for those parts of the line which have now been dismantled, and the present tense for those parts which are still in operation and for structures which, though no longer used for railway purposes, are still standing. Numbers within brackets are grid references on the Ordnance Survey 1:50,000 maps of Great Britain, the maps concerned being Nos. 49, 50, 51 and 57.

After leaving Callander station (7082 2626) the line ran behind St Andrew's Episcopal Church and Rectory and then swung leftwards, passing under the road to Strathyre and Lochearnhead (the present A84) and then over the river Balvaig just before its junction with the Gobhain (the stream that drains Loch Venachar). After that it made a wide curve to the north-west across flat ground and then climbed for two miles at 1 in 61 through the wooded defile of the Pass of Leny, at the narrowest part of which it crossed and re-crossed the river by bowstring girder bridges before turning to the north and emerging from the Pass on to flatter ground again. At St Bride's Crossing (7098 2584) was the first passing loop, beyond which lay the four-miles-long Loch Lubnaig. The road here takes the east side of the Loch, but the railway kept to the west and remained on level ground close to the water's edge until a mile short of Strathyre village. The view across the loch to the right was a pleasant one, towards the wooded southern spurs of Stuc a Chroin; leftward the ground rose too steeply to afford views except momentarily. After passing an isolated railwayman's house the line curved round a craggy spur of Ardnandave Hill, turned to the north-west and then to the north again, crossed the Balvaig a mile beyond the head of the loch and reached Strathyre station (7170 2560); here one was just nine miles from Callander.

Continuing more or less on the level for a further two miles, the railway reached Kingshouse halt, near the hotel of that name and the branch road that leads up the Balquhidder valley, where trains set down or picked up by request. Continuing near the Lochearnhead road, it turned to the north-east, giving passengers looking back along the train a momentary prospect to the west along the Braes of Balquhidder towards Loch Voil, with the high peak of Stobinian (3,821 ft) visible in clear weather on the distant horizon; it could be seen again later when the train had gone beyond Crianlarich. At Balquhidder Junction ("Lochearnhead" until 1905) (7210 2574) the Caledonian's branch to Comrie, Crieff and Perth, completed in 1905, diverged to the right, falling towards Lochearnhead, curving round to the east across the foot of Glen Ogle over a large stone viaduct (7240 2589) and then following the north shore of Loch Earn and the Earn valley eastwards. The main line of the Callander and Oban, however, now veered to the left and began the long climb at 1 in 60 to its highest point. Ascending steeply upwards along the hillside, crossing the Kendrum burn by a viaduct (7224 2575), passing within a quarter of a mile of Edinchip House, the seat of the chief of the MacGregor clan, it then curved round the nose of Meall Reamhar and climbed along the stone-strewn western flank of Glen Ogle. Along this section the choicest prospect for the traveller was the view down Loch Earn,

Callander station staff posed for camera in 1895. *Courtesy, David and Charles*

A busy scene at Callander Station, 4–6–0 "Black Five" No. 45153 picking up coaches in April 1959 to back on to the 12.05 pm from Oban to Glasgow which is standing at the platform. *H.B. Priestley*

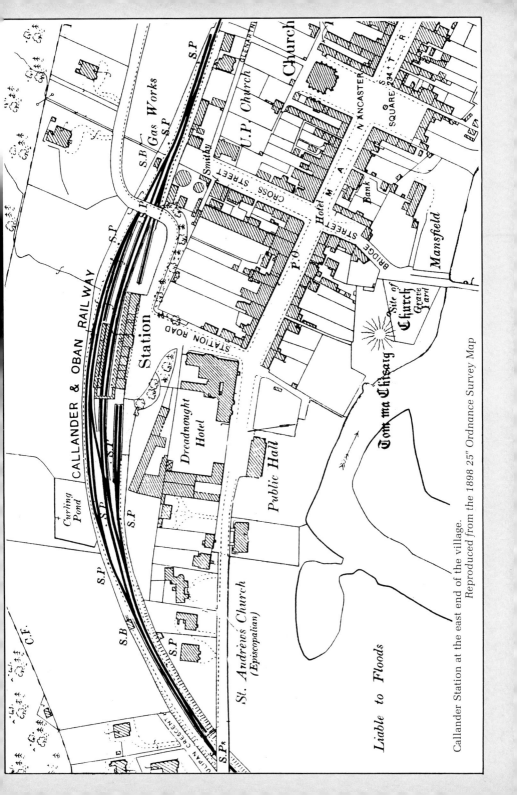

Callander Station at the east end of the village.
Reproduced from the 1898 25" Ordnance Survey Map

Strathyre Station showing the up platform in the 'Thirties.   *Lens of Sutton*

Strathyre Station. The ornamental fountain on the up platform photographed in 1958.
A similar fountain was erected at Dalmally   *Photomatic Ltd.*

The large platform area is well portrayed in this early view of Balquhidder Station, looking south towards Callander. The costume of the many waiting passengers suggests the picture was taken before the First World War. *Real Photographs*

The up platform of Balquhidder Station. This photograph was probably taken after the branch line to Crieff closed in 1951, since the name-board mentions no possible connection. *Lens of Sutton*

A very early postcard view of Balquhidder Station showing the up platform and shelter.
Lens of Sutton

A final view of Balquhidder Station, looking north in the Oban direction on the 3rd April, 1959. "Black Five" No. 45153 takes on water before departing with the 12.05 from Oban to Glasgow.
H.B. Priestley

An early view of Kingshouse halt, the request-stop platform which served the near-by Kingshouse Hotel.   *Lens of Sutton*

A view of Loch Earn and of Lochearnhead village and viaduct (with branch train) taken from a train climbing from Balquhidder to Glenoglehead; June 1951.
                                                                        H.C. Casserley

Glenoglehead platform photographed in August 1961 looking in the direction of Oban. This was the highest point reached by the line 940 feet above datum and the unique signal box is worthy of study as is the tablet-exchanger situated in a dip in the platform.   *H.B. Priestley*

A further view of Glenoglehead platform with the signalman having just passed the tablet to the train.   *H.C. Casserley*

Luib Station, looking west towards Oban. *Lens of Sutton*

The unusual construction of Luib signal cabin seen here from the train in 1958.
Photomatic Ltd

the loch and its shores being viewed almost as if from an aircraft. Further on, and looking downwards, one saw the road that led up Glen Ogle across to Glen Dochart, a thin ribbon of grey (thinner than it is now). Beneath it, closer to the Ogle burn, could be seen the grassy remnants of the road made by General Wade in the early eighteenth century, to open up the Highlands for Government troops after the first Jacobite rebellion of 1715.

This part of the line had been difficult to construct. Stone retaining walls were needed in a number of places, together with two viaducts, one short and one much longer (7262 2573) across gullies. In several places the consequences could (and still can) be seen of rock falls, fragments split from the crag faces above during periods of severe frost. This particular stretch of line was the toughest that any Oban-bound train had to face. Even a powerful "Black Five" 4–6–0 in London Midland and Scottish days did well to top the summit with a six-coach train without falling below twenty miles an hour. At Glenoglehead (7285 2558) the climb ended. Edwardian guidebooks rather ridiculously compared this spot with the Khyber Pass on the Indian North-West Frontier, for the supposed savagery of its scenery; "sylvan" would be a better word to describe Lochan nan Eala and its wooded shores. Here, at the site of the original "Killin" station, there was a crossing loop and a single small platform occasionally used by railway employees.

The line soon curved to the west and descended obliquely across the southern slopes of Glen Dochart, crossing the Ardchyle burn (7287 2523) and Ledcharrie burn (7273 2507) by substantial stone viaducts. Two miles from Glenoglehead the Killin branch came steeply up from the north-east to join the main line at Killin Junction (7289 2532), a sizeable station which merely existed so that travellers could change trains to and from Killin; nothing now remains of it except for a few lumps of earth. Reaching valley level at Luib (7277 2493) in Glen Dochart, where there was a station and passing loop, the line continued more or less on the level to Crianlarich. Views now became more constricted, the valley narrowing almost to a gorge before reaching Loch Iubhair. Here the line ran close under the huge mass of Ben More, the highest hill anywhere near the line along the whole of its course, 3,843 ft high. Across Loch Iubhair are the hills dividing Glen Dochart from Glen Lochay, which include some lesser Munros. These were then lost sight of as the glen narrowed and the railway passed along the southern shore of Loch Dochart, which contains an island bearing a picturesque ruin (7257 2406) miscalled a castle but actually once a house with a wide chimney standing up like a tower.

Turning round to the right to face up the wide valley of Strathfillan, the route reached Crianlarich. Here was Crianlarich Lower station, which as first built had two platforms and a passing loop, but which, when the loop was moved further to the west, lost its up platform. Half a mile further on the spur from the West Highland line comes down on the left to join the Callander and Oban, just after the latter passes under the first of two high viaducts which carry the main line of the West Highland Railway across Strathfillan. The junction itself (7256 2381), though now a mere joining of the main Oban branch with a remnant of the Callander and Oban which remains as a siding, was originally a more complicated affair with as many

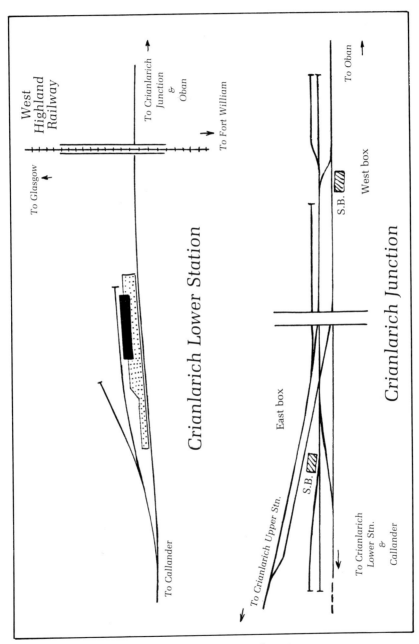

West Highland Railway

To Glasgow

To Crianlarich Junction & Oban

To Fort William

Crianlarich Lower Station

To Callander

To Oban

West box

S.B.

East box

S.B.

To Crianlarich Upper Stn.

To Crianlarich Lower Stn. & Callander

Crianlarich Junction

Diagrammatic station layouts

A view of Luib Station in August 1961 looking this time towards Callander.

H.B. Priestley

Crianlarich Upper Junction in 1936. The line diverging to the right is the main West Highland line to Fort William and that to the left is the spur which sloped steeply down to join the main Callander and Oban line after the latter had passed under the West Highland line.When this picture was taken trains seldom used the spur; now it is the beginning of the Oban branch which thus starts at Crianlarich Upper Station.

Photomatic Ltd

Looking along the line in 1973 towards Crianlarich Lower Station and on to Callander. The carriage (whose windows are on the right) is standing on the spur line from the Upper Station at Crianlarich. *H.C. Casserley*

An unusual visitor in July 1951 to Crianlarich Lower Station. A Lancashire & York-shire coach built in 1894, standing in a siding behind Crianlarich Lower Station. This coach was used by the Departmental Section and numbered DM 198569. It was a Brake Third, 49 ft long, with 5 compartments, built to Diagram D33 in order A10, and was withdrawn in 1954. *H.C. Casserley*

Crianlarich Lower Station. The down platform, photographed in July 1931 after the demolition of the up platform. The viaduct behind carries the West Highland line from Crianlarich Upper Station to Fort William. *H.C. Casserley*

Crianlarich Station, as originally built, with its two platforms, and showing the tablet-catcher on the left. *Lens of Sutton*

A 'Black Five' No. 45499 starts a train in the Oban direction from Crianlarich Lower Station in June 1951 and is about to pass under the West Highland line.

H.C. Casserley

Tyndrum Station photographed from the up platform, looking west towards Oban.

Lens of Sutton

Tyndrum Station, looking westwards towards Oban in August 1961.   *H.B. Priestley*

Dalmally Station, looking eastwards towards Callander. This view clearly shows the shed tucked away behind the Station.   *Lens of Sutton*

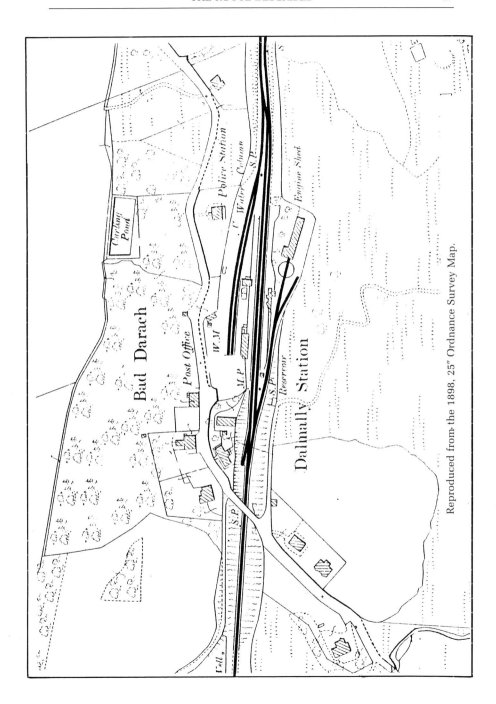

Bud Darach

Dalmally Station

Curling Pond

Police Station

C. Water Column

S.B.

Engine Shed

Post Office

W.M.

M.P.

L.S.P.

Reservoir

S.P.

Well

Reproduced from the 1898, 25" Ordnance Survey Map.

Dalmally Station, looking this time westwards towards Oban. The engine shed is behind the Station buildings on the left. *Real Photographs*

Loch Awe Station, looking eastwards towards Callander. The woman passenger's costume suggests a date *c.*1910. Note also the newsagent's bookstall which seems well stocked for such a small Station. *Real Photographs*

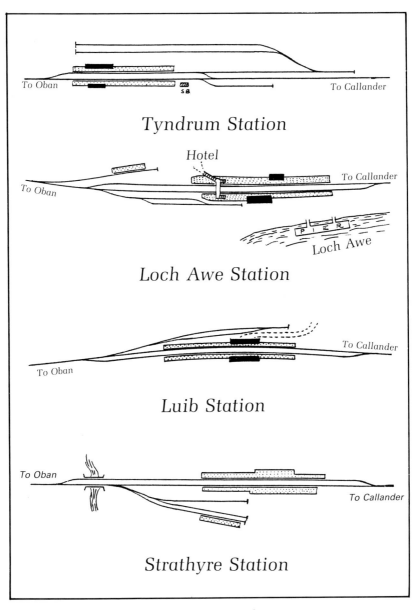

Tyndrum Station

Loch Awe Station

Luib Station

Strathyre Station

Diagrammatic station layouts

as four lines running parallel between two signal boxes. Crianlarich itself is a road junction of some importance – one finds it signposted as much as fifty miles away. It began to attract inhabitants when the Callander and Oban railway arrived; more came when the West Highland railway arrived. From that time onwards most of the local employment was provided by the two lines. Crianlarich has considerable tourist potential but no real attempt has yet been made to develop it as a place for mountain sports, though close at hand there are some magnificent hills.

From the junction onwards the line is still in use. Between Crianlarich and Tyndrum it keeps the river Fillan on its right, at some little distance, climbing gently at first and then more steeply at 1 in 72/61 towards Tyndrum. Across Strathfillan to the north the course of the West Highland line can be clearly traced as it climbs along the northern side of the valley towards Tyndrum Upper station. The last two miles of the Callander and Oban form a great curve, first to the west and then to the north, crossing the Fillan just short of its origin where the Coninish and Dubhcraig burns unite (7285 2334). To the right there are views of high hills, culminating in Ben Chaluim and Ben Odhar, one a Munro and the other nearly so; to the left, a mile short of Tyndrum, one has a good view of the crags of Ben Lui (3,709 ft) and in the glen leading towards it deposits of gold ore have recently been found well below ground level. There is talk of exploiting them; the casual searcher, however, need not expect to discover any nuggets.

Tyndrum Lower station (7301 2327) is about three-quarters of a mile from the County March between Perthshire and Argyllshire. Beyond it there is a short pitch at 1 in 49, the steepest gradient on the whole line before the summit on the county boundary at 840 ft above the sea. To the left, on the hillside, are disused lead-mine workings where, so rumour goes, there are deposits of uranium; one hopes it is merely a rumour. The subsequent descent into Glen Lochy is at first gradual and the surroundings are dull and featureless. The line keeps close to the Tyndrum-Oban road for some six miles; along this stretch trains and cars frequently race one another, and since the line is subject to a general limit of 60 mph the cars often win. Just beyond the summit a small and dullish piece of water, Lochan nan Bi, is passed on the left; its only claim to importance it that it holds (they say locally) the best curling stones in Scotland. Five and three-quarter miles from Tyndrum Glenlochy crossing loop formerly existed (7294 2254) but is now no longer there. Just under three miles further on the line diverges from the road to the south and begins to descend steeply, in places at 1 in 50, passing through numerous cuttings and recent conifer plantations and across three girder bridges, and curving a great deal. Dalmally (7270 2161) is reached twelve miles beyond Tyndrum.

A mile beyond Dalmally the line flattens out and crosses the wide strath of the Orchy just before the latter enters Loch Awe. Here is a seven-span girder bridge (7281 2137) which is the longest on the whole route. To the right are Glen Strae and a cluster of high summits; to the left, on a piece of flat ground jutting into the north-east corner of the Loch, is the impressive ruin of Kilchurn castle, once a Campbell stronghold, the subject of one of Words-worth's effusions. Romantic in appearance, now uninhabited and owl-

The picturesque position of the Falls of Cruachan Halt, looking westwards towards Oban.

Lens of Sutton

Loch Awe Station, looking westwards towards Oban.

Real Photographs

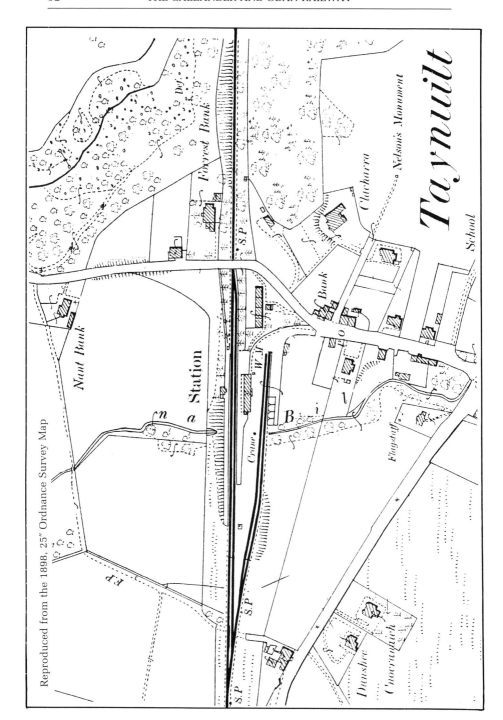

Taynuilt Station, signal box and water column looking east towards Callander. The peak faintly visible in the background is the western summit of Ben Cruachan.

Real Photographs

Taynuilt Station, looking westwards towards Oban photographed in the 'Thirties. Note the very ornate valance canopy boards. *Real Photographs*

The picturesque Ach-na-Cloich Halt, looking westwards towards Oban.
Real Photographs

An earlier view of Ach-na-Cloich Halt this time looking eastwards towards Callander.
Lens of Sutton

Connel Ferry Station showing the down island platform, looking east. "Black Five" No. 45158 *Glasgow Yeomanry* stands at the head of the 7.50 am from Glasgow. It has just crossed with the mid-day train from Oban to Glasgow, seen disappearing in the distance on 30th August, 1961.   *H.B. Priestley*

In this pre-First World War photograph we can see the Oban ticket platform viewed looking towards Oban Station. The locomotive is a 4–6–0 Oban Bogie "Mark II" engine, No. 53, in Caledonian livery. Note the small gasholder on the right.
Real Photographs

A good view of Oban Junction signal box. *Photomatic Ltd*

Pickersgill Oban Bogie "Mark III" 4-6-0 No. 14260 passing under the Caledonian signal gantry near Oban ticket platform in June 1927. *H.C. Casserley*

The very large engine shed at Oban.   *Real Photographs*

The ticket platform at Oban, looking towards Callander. Photographed in April 1952 it shows the signal box and very tall signals beyond the bridge.   *H.C. Casserley*

An old postcard view of the interior of Oban Station, before its enlargement by the addition of extra platforms. Note the profusion of advertisement hoardings, flower baskets and the gas lamps.

Lens of Sutton

The 4.55 pm train with No. 55263 in charge about to leave Oban for Ballachulish. Probably photographed in the 'Fifties.

H.C. Casserley

The fine clock tower and "balanced" buildings of Oban Station.   *Real Photographs*

Trains about to leave Oban in 1905. *Left*, an Oban Bogie "Mark I"; *right*, an Oban Bogie "Mark II". *Note*: the new platforms had been added by this time.   *Lens of Sutton*

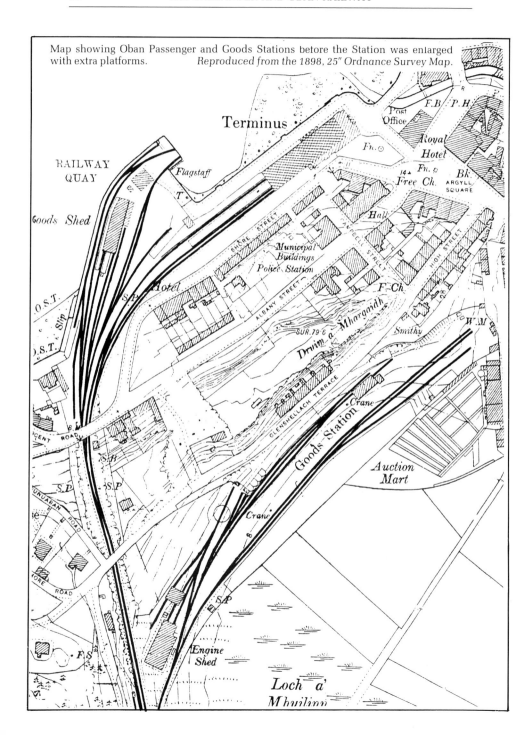

Map showing Oban Passenger and Goods Stations before the Station was enlarged with extra platforms. *Reproduced from the 1898, 25" Ordnance Survey Map.*

A panoramic view of Oban Station and harbour showing the track layout and photographed probably in the 'Fifties. *Pendon Museum*

An aerial view of Oban goods Station photographed in June 1927. This photograph shows the engine shed, turntable and auction market well. *H.C. Casserley*

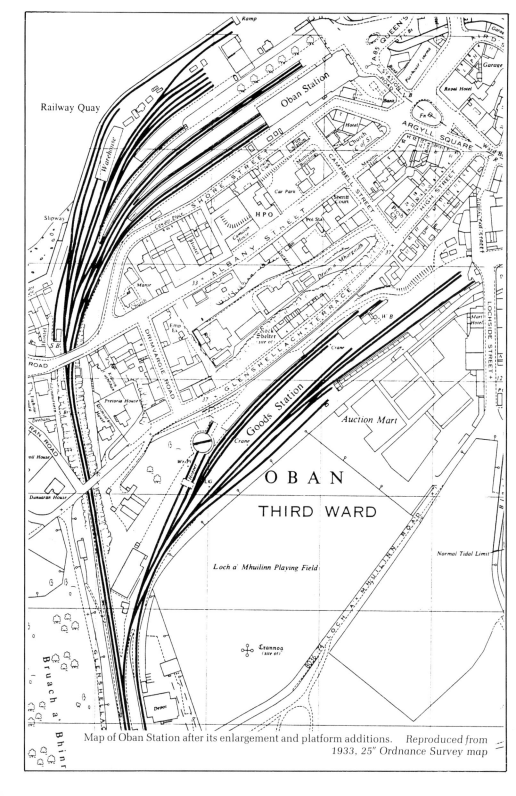

Map of Oban Station after its enlargement and platform additions. Reproduced from 1933, 25″ Ordnance Survey map

ridden, it is worth examining through binoculars as the train swings round it in a 90 degree arc. Beyond it, as one looks back across the loch, is Ben Lui's impressive summit, now ten miles away, and the sharp little peak of Ben Buie further to the south, one of the least visited of the Scottish Munros since it is so far from any road.

The line now runs alongside the northern V-shaped shore of Loch Awe for some eight miles, keeping near the water's edge most of the way; the road to Oban is in close attendance. To the right is the huge mass of Ben Cruachan, too near for its summits to be visible; to the left is an extensive panoramic view of the broad northern end of the loch, studded with islands. At Loch Awe station (7274 2124) is the pier that was constructed when the line was built, now in use again after many years of idleness during the summer season, when a small launch cruises around the northern end of the loch, carrying sightseers.

The line continues along Loch Awe, keeping more or less level. Many rock cuttings show that this was by no means an easy stretch to construct. It rises slightly to cross the bridge over the outflow from the ravine where the Falls of Cruachan can be briefly seen as the train passes them; a platform was placed here in 1922 and one train each way stopped there daily for visitors who wished to get out and inspect them. The platform was disused in 1940 but has recently been re-opened. Loch Awe now narrows into the Pass of Brander, and here one reaches a unique safety mechanism, a fence of parallel wires on the north side of the line designed to stop rocks falling on to the railway; this is described more completely in Appendix Two. A little further on the route bears to the left to cross the river Awe by a girder bridge high above the water (7301 2021) and then continues along the west bank of that river before turning to reach Taynuilt, a two-platform station still very much the same as when it was built (7312 2003).

After Taynuilt the line goes beneath the main Oban road, runs parallel with it for rather more than half a mile and then turns sharply north, following the line of a burn, to the shore of Loch Etive. Half a mile further on is the pier of Ach-na-Cloich, where there was formerly a one-platform halt whose buildings are still standing; here some of the trains stopped to connect with tourist vessels plying on the loch. Across the water, just under half a mile distant from the line, is Ardchattan House, beside which are the ruins of a Priory, founded in 1230 in what must have been at the time an extraordinarily remote spot. The remains are too slight to be picked out with binoculars but are worth a visit. Ardchattan House is largely built with stones from the ruined buildings.

Beyond Ach-na-Cloich the line turns south again to cross the Oban road at right angles and then curves round and keeps fairly close to both the road and the shoreline until Connel Ferry is reached. (7340 2916) Along this part of the line the views toward the hills on the opposite side of Loch Etive and (if the weather is clear enough) across the Moss of Achnacree to the mountains of Morven are rewarding. The climax comes as the cantilever bridge at Connel (described in Appendix One) comes into sight. Connel Ferry is a cluster of hotels and houses, together with (more recently) an oil storage yard beside the station, which is now a shadow of its former self and a mere unstaffed halt.

It was originally intended that the line west of Connel should more or less follow the shore and reach Oban from the north-east. Landowners' objections necessitated a more inland course. Immediately on leaving Connel the line climbs on a gradient steepening to 1 in 50 and curves inland towards a low pass in the hills above the head of Glen Cruitten. The summit is reached at what was formerly a crossing place with a large signal box and signalmen's houses in a cutting between rock walls (7310 2882). The line now makes its final descent, three miles at 1 in 50, curving a sinuous path along the southern side of Glen Cruitten as it loses height, and eventually swinging right round to enter Oban from the south-west in a great sickle-shaped curve. After passing through a gash cut in a ridge of rock the line sent off a divergence to the right, to a goods yard; another branch to the left led to the railway quay. The main track then fanned out into the station platforms at Oban and so reached its terminus, 71 miles from Callander.

The line's first Engineer, Mr Blyth, had prophesied that the finished line would be the most beautiful in Scotland. It is not quite that; the Mallaig extension of the West Highland line surely claims that distinction, but one may allow second equal place with the Dingwall and Kyle line for the Callander and Oban. Except for a few miles in Glen Lochy it is never dull, always scenic, and in places a continuous belvedere for miles on end. Even now, reduced to four-sevenths of its former size, it is worth journeying on for the views it affords, and most of the disused three-sevenths can still be enjoyed by vigorous walkers.

The two span bridge across the narrows of Loch Creran, on the Ballachulish branch line. *Author*

Chapter Seven
Stations, Signalling and Permanent Way

At the time when the Callander and Oban line was at its busiest and most active, just prior to the outbreak of World War I, it had fifteen stations – sixteen if one includes Glenoglehead, which was not open to the public but served a few of the company's employees. Of all these stations Oban was the largest. So far as long distance traffic went, it had almost as many departures and arrivals in the course of a summer weekday as Marylebone in London, and there were also five trains in each direction serving the Ballachulish branch. Callander, though not as large as Oban, was even busier; as well as the through trains to the west it was the terminus for ten in each direction from and to Glasgow and Edinburgh, some of which contained through portions from the latter city that were attached to Oban trains.

Callander was, next to Oban, the largest centre of population on the line. The Dunblane, Doune and Callander branch, which had briefly been part of the Scottish Central system before being taken over by the Caledonian, had terminated several hundred yards east of the Callander and Oban line's station which, at the request of local people, had been sited just behind the Dreadnought Hotel. From the latter the C&O had put out a short eastern extension to join the DD&C a little way east of the latter's terminus, which now became redundant and was used as a goods terminal.

The Callander and Oban's first station had been small, with one platform of average size and one very short, but in 1883 it was reconstructed. Like all the company's other stations except one its upper structures were of painted timber. It had a long facade facing the station forecourt where carriages connected with trains to take visitors into the Trossachs. This was of great length and had elaborately sculptured eaves and three gabled transepts, one at each end and a larger one in the centre above the main entrance. The structure behind it contained the usual station offices, including a news vendor's stand and a buffet, and gave access to the down platform. Both main platforms, on either side of the double track loop, were on a gentle curve. A passenger footbridge across the tracks linked them; until 1947 this bridge was crowned centrally by a small clock tower, but an unfortunate accident brought about the bridge's destruction (see Chapter 12) and a new one was then put up without any clock. North of the up platform a double loop ran for non-stopping traffic, and there were bays at either end of both up and down platforms.

Strathyre station, 9 miles further on, had originally only one platform. A fire destroyed it in 1893 and it was then rebuilt with two, with timber superstructures and the main entry from the up platform towards the road; this platform also had a water tower at the southern end. The picturesque nature of the village seems to have inspired the station staff to make their charge attractive, and much time was spent in ornamenting it with shrubs on both platforms and a lineside garden having rockeries, rustic gateways and a fountain carved from granite in the shape of a heron with an upward-pointing beak through which the water spouted. Similar heron-fountains were also placed at two other stations on the line. Strathyre station has now vanished completely but the garden, with the heron, is still there. Next along

A good study of the main line and shunting signal at Connel Ferry, photographed in 1958.

Photomatic Ltd

The all-wooden Strathyre signal cabin, with a camping coach in the bay just beyond.

Photomatic Ltd

the line was Kingshouse halt, a single unstaffed platform made entirely of wood at the expense of the adjacent Kingshouse Hotel in 1871; trains stopped here when timely notice was given to the guard by passengers wishing to alight, or when a hand signal was made from the platform. Of Kinghouse, too, no vestige remains.

The station which was later called Balquhidder Junction began as a single platform known as Lochearnhead (though it was more than 2 miles away from that village). It retained that name till 1905, when the Caledonian's new branch which linked Perth with Crieff, Comrie and St Fillans along the Earn valley extended itself southwards round the head of Loch Earn to link up with the Callander and Oban. The station now became a junction and was reconstructed with three platform faces, two being on either side of an island platform; access from the adjacent road was by an underpass and up stairways. Here connections were made between the main line and the branch. The latter actually provided the quickest way from Perth to Oban and vice versa, although there were no through vehicles. Here too, as at Strathyre, there was a water tower, near the down starting signal. The branch, however, did not have a very long life. It was closed in 1951, and for the next fourteen years Balquhidder was a mere unstaffed halt, becoming more and more dismal and untidy; its two signal boxes were removed; it became once more the nearest station to Lochearnhead, but now that Alexanders' buses were serving that village there were probably few to use the train. The station lingered on until the line closed in 1965. All that now remains of it is the under-pass entry from the road, blocked by a fence.

Seven-and-a-half miles beyond Balquhidder was Killin Junction, also serving a branch and having no *raison d'etre* except to do so. It was constructed when the Killin branch (described in the next chapter) was built. It had a single down platform on the southern side and a two-faced island platform on the opposite side of the passing loop. The train plying to and from Killin left from or returned to the northern face of the island platform, and a footbridge connected the down and up platform faces. The usual timber buildings naturally included no booking office; indeed, there were no houses near and not even a metalled access road. Here one might have to wait three-quarters of an hour for a connection if one were unlucky. It too, with its tall signal box in the angle between the main line and the branch, has now disappeared completely.

Luib, 3½ miles further on, was a station of the same 2-platform pattern as Strathyre, with a shelter on the down side of the passing loop and more substantial buildings on the up side. While not as isolated as Killin Junction it must have had very few patrons for there is no village in the vicinity and very few houses. It too has now vanished and the site is covered with caravans whose owner and hirer lives in the former station master's house.

At Crianlarich, some 6½ miles further on, one comes to a village of about the same size as Strathyre. From 1894 to 1965 it enjoyed the distinction of having two railway stations, the Upper one on the West Highland line and the Lower one on the Callander and Oban. The latter's station was not impressive; originally a two-platform affair like Strathyre and Luib, it lost the up platform when the passing loop was moved half a mile to the west after the line to Fort William was built, so as to be beyond the spur from the latter. Crianlarich had quite a profusion of sidings, and these, together with a half-mile length of the line itself, still remain and are in regular use, receiving timber wagons which are loaded here with tree trunks from nearby forests brought in by lorries; they are then taken away by rail, being shunted along the line and up the spur.

Tyndrum, for a while the terminus of the line, though merely a couple of platforms on either side of a passing loop, with no substantial structures on them, had originally a number of sidings, together with a turntable and engine shed. The two latter were removed when the line was continued to Dalmally. The sidings remained till 1965. The space they occupied is now, as Luib, a caravan park; the down platform has gone and the up platform has a small shelter; it has become an unstaffed halt; the passing loop has also been removed.

Dalmally, 12 miles further on, was the one example on the Callander and Oban of a station whose buildings were of stone – actually red sandstone. On the up platform these remain much as when they were built in 1877; the down platform, on the other hand, has had its shelter demolished, and there is no longer any overbridge connecting the platforms. The down platform still bears a granite heron-fountain similar to the one at Strathyre, though it no longer spouts water. Outside the station on the up side there is a sizeable fore-court, from which, during the three years' interval, 1877–1880, coaches left connecting with the trains during the time when Dalmally was the terminus of the line. From the eastern approach to the station points led to sidings north of the up platform which finished just short of the fore-court; on the other side there were also a turntable and engine shed; all these latter have now vanished. The signal box, though still there, on the up platform, is no longer operative since the new radio-signalling method came into operation in 1985.

Loch Awe station, on the north side of the northern arm of Loch Awe itself and close to the hotel of the same name, had two platforms on either side of a passing loop, and gave access not only to the hotel and village but also to the pier. From here steamers operated on the loch, traversing its whole length as far as the village of Ford at the upper end, connecting there with coach services to Lochgilphead and the other places in that area. The station had its quota of sidings and most trains stopped at it. Loch Awe is the only station on the part of the line which is still open for traffic which was closed and later re-opened in response to local demand. It is now a single-platform unstaffed halt, and the former passing loop has gone; the space where the sidings were is now a car park where owners can leave their vehicles if they wish to go on a boat trip from the pier. The former service to Ford has long been discontinued but a launch cruises on the north end of the loch during the summer.

Next along the line was the single platform built at the end of World War I for would-be sightseers coming to look at the Falls of Cruachan, a spectacular cascade which here falls down the side of Ben Cruachan on its way into Loch Awe. Some trains stopped there in both directions. The platform had a short life; it was used no more after 1939. However, three years ago it was experimentally re-opened and trains halt there on request.

Taynuilt signal cabin at the end of the down platform, ground situated, photographed in 1973. *H.C. Casserley*

Kentallen signal cabin, this time mounted on the platform. Note the fine oil lamp. *H.C. Casserley*

The tall, brick-built Killin Junction signal box, situated between the lines. *H.C. Casserley*

Taynuilt, a large village 9 miles beyond Loch Awe station and pier, was a station of the standard two-platform type with very extensive timber buildings on the down platform and a sizeable shelter on the opposite side; it also had a substantially-built water-tower. Both platforms are still used, though not equally, the down platform frequently receiving trains going in the direction of Callander. The up platform has lost its former wooden shelter, which has been replaced by a small glass one. There are two goods sidings on the south side which are still much in use. Over the main entrance door to the station on the south side, is a badge with the inscription "C. and O." and the date of construction in Roman numerals, the only remaining sign of the former company left on the system.

The remains of the buildings and platform at the former halt at Ach-na-Cloich, a little further on, are still to be seen, as also is the pier; boats still ply from the latter on Loch Etive, but no longer in connection with the trains, which ceased to call in 1965.

Connel Ferry, the last station before Oban, has come up in the world and then gone down again. Originally a two-platform affair serving the village of Connel, with the main timber buildings on the up platform and a shelter on the down side, it resembled other stations on the line. However, when the branch to Ballachulish was opened in 1903, it was considerably extended. The down platform was reconstructed as an island, and trains on the branch ran through to its southern face to connect with services to or from the east before proceeding to Oban or Ballachulish. Connel Ferry became an important junction. The main up platform was also given a bay at either end, so that there were five platforms in all. A Caledonian Railway-style footbridge was also built, linking the up and down platforms. Now the glory has departed; the branch line is disused, only the old up platform still remains, and this has lost all its buildings. A small glass shelter serves to protect passengers from inclement weather, and a small wooden gate gives access from the village. Behind the up platform, where formerly there were railway sidings, an oil storage depot has been established, it too has its own sidings which receive oil wagons daily from the down afternoon goods train.

The chief station on the line has always been Oban. When first built it had three platforms and it was later enlarged by the provision of two more between the earlier building and the quayside. Oban station was among the most distinctive buildings in the town, with its prominent clock tower crowned by a small spire. The concourse, under glass, was spacious enough to have accommodated the town's whole population at the time when it was built. Even the public lavatories were spacious. There was a sizeable newsstand where every periodical one could think of was displayed, either on the stand itself or on trestle tables in front. A small buffet served basic fare at reasonable prices. The whole structure was built of timber and glass, and must have been a terrible fire risk, but it survived until 1985, by which time no trains were using the three original platforms but only the two outside ones that had been added later. It was far too large for late twentieth century traffic and had become a blue-and-white elephant taking up space that could be profitably disposed of.

It was decided to build a new station, and in 1985 this was opened. It was sited at the buffer-ends of the two outside platforms. A square brick box,

Lochawe signal box, of concrete construction. Note the splendid flowing design of the lattice footbridge. *Lens of Sutton*

Crianlarich junction half a mile west of Crianlarich Lower Station. To the right is the spur-line from Crianlarich Upper Station. *H.C. Casserley*

fawn-coloured with a low tiled roof, it is neat but not gaudy, and there is not much room inside in which to shelter from the rain. There is no buffet; toilet accommodation is cramped, though at present commendably clean and unvandalised; the news-stand is tiny. However, one takes the fact that the place was constructed at all as a good omen for the line's continuance. Once it had been brought into use the old station was doomed. It disappeared in a few weeks during 1987, the smoke from its destruction going up in a dozen spirals from bonfires. It is said that its place will be taken by a leisure centre. It had to go; it could not have been converted into any other sort of building. But one misses it, when one looks across the town to see what the time is, from a vanished clock. A landmark has gone for ever. It is all very sad.

The method of signalling employed on the line was the Electric Token Block System, commonly used on most single lines in Britain which could not simply be run on the principle of "one engine in steam." At each station or passing loop the signal box worked on the principle that only one train was permitted on each section of the line at any one time in between passing places. Only when the signalman had ascertained that the whole of the next section was clear, through sending a message by bell-code to the next box and receiving an affirmative bell-code signal in reply, could the tablet be removed from the dispensing instrument in the box which gave the driver of the train permission to proceed – and that tablet itself could not be taken out until the one already handed to the signalman by the driver was inserted into the apparatus. Points were then set and signals ahead lowered, and the train proceeded. This was the general practice, though the rule book provided for slight variations in certain contingencies. Since only one train could be on a single-line section, collisions were impossible.

This method worked satisfactorily for over a hundred years, but it was expensive in its use of labour and required miles and miles of signal-wiring and point-rodding, which needed maintenance and which could be put out of action in severe weather conditions. A drastic simplification has recently taken place on the portion of the Oban line which is still open. All signals have been removed, signal boxes have been stripped of their levers; most points are now worked by hand if in sidings, or on the line itself are set for the left-hand loop at a crossing, by a spring setting. When a train comes from the direction which makes a particular switch a trailing point, the train's wheels push the switch blade back so that the train is not derailed; after it has passed the blades spring back again. Only at one point on the line are points set from a signal box – at Crianlarich Upper station, where a push-button appliance in what was once the signal box can move them elec-trically one way or the other, for Fort William or Oban trains, as necessary.

Such former signal boxes on the line as still remained open – Dalmally, Taynuilt and Oban – are really now depots whence tokens are issued. When a train arrives a member of the station staff replaces one token and removes the next from the instrument holding them and gives a verbal instruction to the waiting driver that replaces the visual instruction previously given by the moveable semaphore signal. A fixed white board with an orange-red spot in the centre and an instruction beneath to stop and await permission to proceed, fixed at driver's eye-level, faces the driver of a train entering a station from either direction and acts as a warning. All trains in any case stop at every station, both the staffed and unstaffed ones. At Crianlarich Upper station this simple system is somewhat modified, however, as it is there that the Oban line branches off from the line to Fort William, so a driver approaching from the Oban direction would have no means of knowing that a train was already blocking his route into the station, if such were the case. Instead of leaving a movable semaphore signal to give this information, which would have been the only one left on the line, the authorities devised a means of giving verbal warning by radio. At some point between Tyndrum and Crianlarich the driver of each train in the Glasgow direction enquires from Crianlarich box through a "walkie-talkie" apparatus as to whether he may enter the station and receives a reply. If the latter is in the negative he brings his train to a halt at a "Stop-board" a quarter of a mile from Crianlarich junction and waits there for permission to be given.

The savings of cost made possible by the scrapping of the former elaborate systems of levers and wires has of course been considerable, and a factor favouring the line's continued viability. The new system is no less safe than the old one so long as drivers understand and obey verbal instructions as they would have done visual signals. Equally, there has been no slowing-down or lessening of the train service. The trains are seldom delayed, though this may occasionally happen at the approach to Crianlarich, but with powerful diesel locomotives hauling light trains there is no difficulty in recouping even ten minutes of lost time south of the latter station.

At one place only semaphore signals are still to be found. This is on a two-mile stretch along the north side of the Pass of Brander, between Loch Awe and Taynuilt stations, where the dangers of boulders rolling down the steep hillside and obstructing the passage of trains were quite early made evident, as related below in Chapter 12. Following a suggestion made by John Anderson, the line's engineers established a very elaborate mechanical safety device in March 1882, in which a wire fence was fixed along the north side of the track to hold back falling rocks. If one of the fence-wires broke, signals were set at danger and no trains could proceed in either direction until inspection had shown the track was clear. This device, "Anderson's Piano", as it was colloquially termed, is fully described below in Appendix Two.

The permanent way between Callander and Oban was originally made up with 24 ft rails, and these remained in use for a long while. Trains travelling over them must have made a noise resembling a rifle-fusillade. Eventually longer rails were put in when replacements were needed, and the original larchwood sleepers gave place to creosote-impregnated ones as used elsewhere. The whole line is now made up of rails 60 ft long except where there are points or sidings, and the former chaired bull-head rails are being replaced when renewals become necessary by heavier flat-bottomed rails with Pandrol clip-fastenings of the now standard type.

A relic of the past, photographed when new. Note the capacity, painted at the bottom left hand corner, in tons, hundredweights and quarters.

Courtesy, H.M.R.S. Collection

Killin Junction Station with its different style footbridge seen here looking towards Callander on 12th July, 1957.

Courtesy, H.M.R.S. Collection

Chapter Eight
The Killin Branch and the
Unbuilt Branch to the Trossachs

During the first quarter of a century after the Callander and Oban Railway reached Oban it acquired two branch lines which together added nearly 33 miles to its total extent. The first to be built was a line to Killin village, at the head of Loch Tay. It took five years to bring it into being, years of alternating expectation and disillusion. The expectations arose chiefly in Killin, through the Marquess of Breadalbane, one of the Callander and Oban's Directors, who lived at Taymouth Castle a mile from the lower end of Loch Tay, was a keen promoter of the line, and more than any other individual person helped to bring it into existence.

As has already been noticed, Killin had had to make do since 1870 with a station bearing its name but actually sited 4 miles away, up the hillside at the head of Glen Ogle. The inconvenience was disliked locally and pressure for a genuine rail link began to mount. During the 1870s the only available ways of reaching Killin and its scenic attractions, which included an impressively cascading river resembling the famous Bettws-y-Coed Falls in North Wales, were by road along the north side of Loch Tay, where horse-drawn coaches plied, and by steamer sailing on the loch itself from Kenmore at its lower end to a pier 1½ miles short of Killin village. The Highland Railway had already reached Aberfeldy by a branch from its main line from Perth to Inverness, but the railhead was still some 6 miles short of Kenmore. The Callander and Oban line was actually nearer to the loch than that, but also 600 ft above it at the nearest point. There were hopes of a rail extension from Aberfeldy at least as far as the loch, but when it became evident that this was not going to materialize Lord Breadalbane pressed the Callander and Oban to build a branch from Luib, in Glen Dochart, down that valley to Killin. Had one been built it would have been 8 miles long, and the 4 mile journey by road from the existing Killin station would have been replaced by some 14 miles of rail. There were no centres of population between Luib and Killin from which traffic might have been gained. In the circumstances it is not surprising that Breadalbane's suggestion was turned down. The company had to reckon how much additional tourist traffic might come its way in return for constructional costs of well over £20,000 and preferred to err on the side of caution.

Breadalbane then made a direct approach to the Caledonian, who were somewhat more sympathetic. They were about to submit a Bill to Parliament applying for permission to build a number of new lines, and the proposed Killin branch was included. However, Parliament rejected the whole Bill. It was now up to the people of Killin to see what they could achieve unaided.

The Marquess again took the lead. He contacted John Strain, who had recently been chosen as Engineer for the Callander and Oban line west of Tyndrum, and engaged him to study the terrain between the line of the latter railway and Killin itself. Strain made his investigation, drew his conclusions and reported them. At a public meeting in August 1882 Breadalbane was able to present Strain's considered views. It would, he said, be possible to construct a line from the village which, rising on a very steep

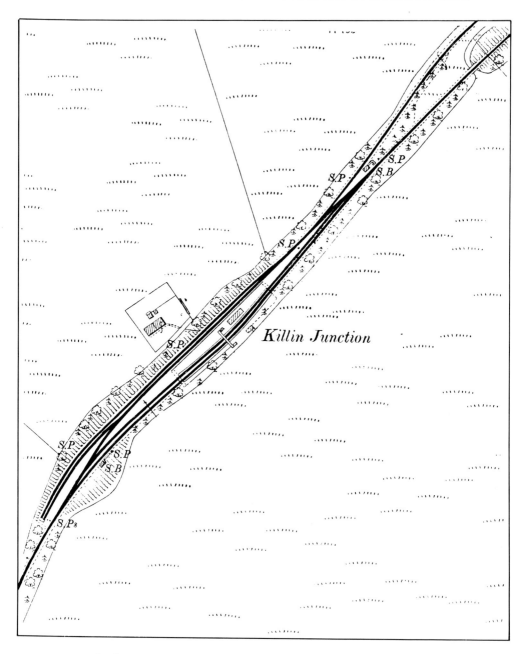

S.P

S.P
S.B

S.P

Killin Junction

S.P

S.P
S.P
S.B

S.P8

Map of Killin Junction. Note the remoteness and absence of any access road.
Reproduced from the 1898, 25″ Ordnance Survey Map

gradient, would link up with the C&O at a point some 2½ miles from the existing Killin station at Glenoglehead. Continuing from the village, a line on level ground could link up with a suitable site for a pier on Loch Tay. The whole would amount to 5½ miles; the cost of building it would be about £18,000; the difference between receipts and running expenses would leave a balance of some £365 to divide between shareholders.

Despite the small expectation of profit the meeting received the Marquess's announcement enthusiastically. One Killin resident offered there and then to invest £1000. Breadalbane himself promised that he himself would add a pound to every pound invested by others. It was taken for granted that the project would go ahead. Parliamentary approval would not be needed since there were no objectors to the scheme. Mr Robertson, manager of the local branch of the Bank of Scotland, was chosen as Secretary. The latter, being well aware of the financial strengths of those who had any money in and around the village, doubted the possibility of raising as much as £18,000, but for the moment enthusiasm was running high, and Breadalbane went so far as to offer to donate the land (all of which ran through his own estates) and to give wood for the sleepers in return for further shares. The Caledonian also offered rails in return for shares, as did also the Callander and Oban, which was feeling more sympathetic towards the whole project now that it was not to be at the expense of building it. John Anderson went so far as the purchase £12,000 worth of shares on his company's behalf. Permission was received from the Board of Trade to construct the line in 1883. The prospects seemed set fair.

Contractors now had to be asked for tenders. Most of them quoted a figure round about what Strain had estimated, but one was markedly less. A Mr MacDonald of Skye offered to do the work for just under £13,800. Strain thought the figure was quite unrealistic, but the promoters found the prospect of saving thousands of pounds irresistible and closed with his offer. However, it was not merely that they wished to save money. The euphoria engendered in the first public meeting was beginning to wane. When asked to put their money where their mouths had been, many began to retract. In the end, when Robertson drew up his estimate of what could be brought in and what would need to be paid out, he found the former fell short of the latter by over £7700.

Nevertheless permission was given to go ahead and work began in the summer of 1883. MacDonald hoped to finish it in less than two years. The actual making of the road bed for the permanent way was a considerable task, requiring the excavation of 100,000 cubic yards of earth by the spades of the navvies. In addition there were two sizeable bridges to be built where the route crossed the rivers Dochart and Lochay on either side of the site for Killin station at the north-eastern end of the village. Strain agreed to a timber bridge for the crossing of the Lochay but insisted that the one over the Dochart had to be of concrete. MacDonald soon began to realize that his tender had been far too low. He made very slow progress because of the economies that his shortage of ready money forced on him, and further discovered that he could not even obtain some of the materials he required unless the Killin Railway underwrote his expenses. By the autumn of 1884

British Railways Standard '4MT' 2-6-4 tank No. 80126 at Killin Junction; June 1963.
H.C. Casserley

Diesel locomotives Nos. 6119 and 6109 on goods train bound for Oban, seen here passing Killin Junction in June 1963. *H.C. Casserley*

0–4–4 tank No. 55195 at Killin Junction in a wintry April 1959.   *H.B. Priestley*

0–6–0 No. 57450 at Killin Junction with the one-coach train which ran on the Killin branch, photographed in April 1952.   *H.C. Casserley*

A bleak view from Killin platform, here facing the Loch Tay end of the line, photographed in July 1957.   H.C. Casserley

0−4−4 tank No. 15103 climbing from Killin Station to Killin Junction with the two-coach branch line train in July 1931.   H.C. Casserley

Killin Station forecourt photographed in June 1962, with the branch line train standing in the platform. *H.C. Casserley*

The Station of Killin with its Station clock, Nestles chocolate machine and seemingly busy atmosphere, in June 1962. Note the line has been re-laid with concrete sleepers. *Lens of Sutton*

he was on the verge of bankruptcy, in a thorough financial muddle, and without the money to pay his men. It began to look as if the line would never be completed.

In December 1884 a new contractor was chosen, John Best of Glasgow, to complete the line; he was advanced £1000 by the promoters and construction re-commenced. A season of bad weather now followed and the summer of 1885 arrived with the task still unfinished. However, it was no longer a matter of whether at all, but of when. John Anderson was now actively interesting himself in the work and was continually in touch with Robertson, giving him advice and encouragement. The latter was anxious to economize as much as possible, and it was agreed that the line should only be worked with one engine. Eventually the rails were placed in position and the junction with the Callander and Oban was laid. In September 1885 Robertson prematurely informed the Board of Trade that the line was finished and ready for inspection, but Strain, who came to see what was going on, insisted it was *not* yet ready and Robertson had to cancel his letter. A second date was fixed, in January 1886, but a fierce snowstorm prevented the Board of Trade Inspector from getting through to Killin. Not till mid-February was approval granted, though in the meantime the line was being unofficially used for transporting coal and hay since the road was blocked by snow.

The official opening ceremony took place on 13th March, 1886, and invitations to attend it were sent to civic bigwigs and senior railway officers in all parts of Scotland. A special train, headed by a Caledonian 0−4−2 tank engine which was almost brand new and in shining blue livery, left Callander during the morning with guests. Meanwhile the Marquess had organized a steamer to bring a party of friends up from Kenmore to the new pier at Loch Tay station, from where another special train composed of a few coaches previously borrowed, carried them over the two bridges and up the 1 in 50 incline to Killin Junction. The passengers met and fraternised on the platform while the two trains were united, then took their seats again and went down the line to Killin, where the customary celebratory meal was eaten and many speeches were made. On 1st April, 1886 the branch was opened for traffic and the former station at Glenoglehead ceased to exist except as a passing place.

The completed line is almost too short to merit description. Leaving Killin Junction from the north side of the island platform, the line descended steadily at 1 in 50 to the north-east, with no deep cuttings or high embankments. Looking forwards and northwards there was a fine mountain prospect of Ben Lawers and its outliers; this mountain is the highest in Scotland outside the Cairngorms and the Ben Nevis massif. Nature raised it to 3984 ft above the sea and a huge man-made cairn just brings it to 4000 ft. The branch avoided the village of Killin, keeping to the south of Dochart and then crossing it obliquely by a concrete viaduct close to the old burying-ground of the MacNab chiefs on an island in the river. A little further on Killin station was reached, a single platform with a wood-and-brick shelter; an engine shed was close by. Crossing the Lochay by a timber bridge, the line now ran level for a further mile, first north and then north-east,

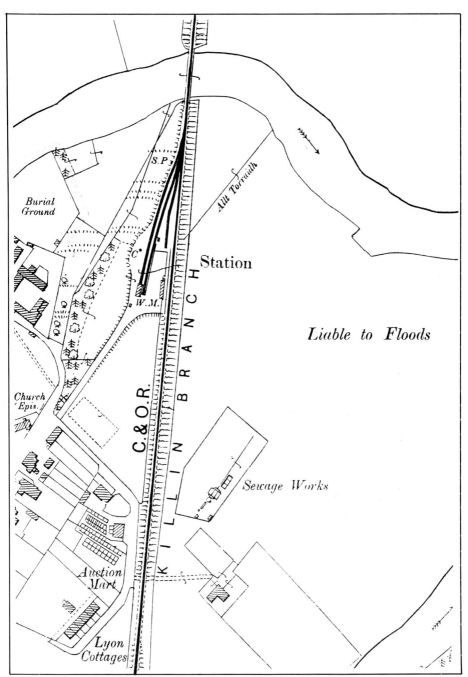

Map showing position of Killin Station situated at the north-eastern end of Killin village. *Reproduced from the 1898, 25" Ordnance Survey Map*

eventually reaching the point where the blunt south-western end of Loch Tay afforded a suitable place for a steamer pier. Loch Tay station was here, a single platform with a looped track that allowed the locomotive to run round its train. The whole of the line's structures have now vanished except for the two bridges and the track bed and the abutments of two road bridges. A large whitewashed public toilet now occupies the site of Killin station; the track bed as far as Loch Tay continues as a footpath but ends before the site of Loch Tay station is reached, merging into the gardens of recently-built houses.

During the autumn of 1870 the possibility of a branch line into the Trossachs had first presented itself. A rumour reached John Anderson's ears that the North British Railway, which had running powers as far as Callander over the branch from Dunblane, were thinking of constructing a line from that branch which would skirt Loch Venachar and reach into the Trossachs – an area becoming a favourite objective for tourists, who travelled there by coach from Callander. Quite apart from its considerable natural beauty, the area was associated with Sir Walter Scott's verse romance *The Lady of the Lake*, which opens with a description of a stag hunt here organized by James IV of Scotland. That the North British should muscle in on Callander and Oban territory was, to Anderson, unthinkable; clearly his own company ought to get in first. So as soon as possible he brought the matter before the Directors, having already himself walked along the whole line of the route where he proposed the branch should run, through land partly owned by the Earl of Moray, partly by the Duke of Montrose. The owner of the Trossachs Hotel near Loch Achray was strongly in favour of Anderson's scheme; the two landowners, approached through their factors, were more lukewarm. The Caledonian Railway made its own estimate of possible extra traffic, which was more pessimistic than Anderson's. The Callander and Oban Board decided to defer consideration of the project, since it was already too late to prepare a Bill in time for the next session of Parliament. At that moment their minds were more concerned about the laggard manner in which the line was being built down Glen Dochart. Soon it appeared that the North British had given up any plans they might have had about a Trossachs branch of their own. So the scheme was dropped, though not by Anderson, who pigeon-holed it in his memory.

Twelve years later it re-appeared. Once more Anderson got wind of a second North British project to send a line into this area. It already had a line linking Glasgow with Aberfoyle and was considering extending it to Callander. This would not only bring Glasgow 8½ miles nearer to that village than by the Caledonian route, but also put the North British in a favourable position to make another branch to the west, south of the proposed Callander terminus, reaching into the Trossachs along the southern shore of Loch Venachar. It was all a matter of rumour, and of hints that came along the grape vine, but Anderson took the possibility seriously and planned to pre-empt it. If any line was to profit from such a venture it should be his own. Tourist traffic between Callander and the Trossachs by road had much increased during the previous ten years, and was carried in

With a few more enamel signs, & a large gas lamp, this view was photographed in July 1931, thirty one years earlier than the one on *page 81*. The branch line train about to leave Killin Station for Killin Junction behind 0−4−4 tank No. 15103.   *H.C. Casserley*

L.M.S. No. 15103 taking on water in front of the engine shed at Loch Tay Station; July 1931.   *H.C. Casserley*

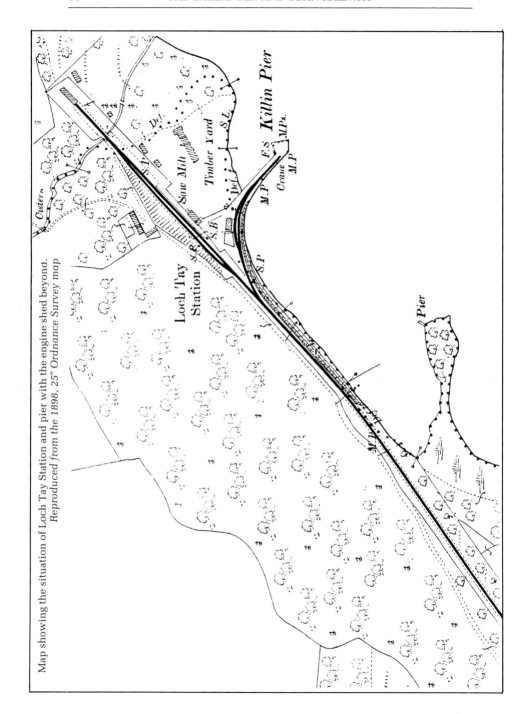

Map showing the situation of Loch Tay Station and pier with the engine shed beyond.
Reproduced from the 1898, 25″ Ordnance Survey map

Loch Tay Station and pier in 1886 with a Killin 'Pug' shunting in the background.
Courtesy, David and Charles

0–4–4 tank No. 15103 at Loch Tay Station in July 1931, looking towards the end of
the line and the engine shed.   *H.C. Casserley*

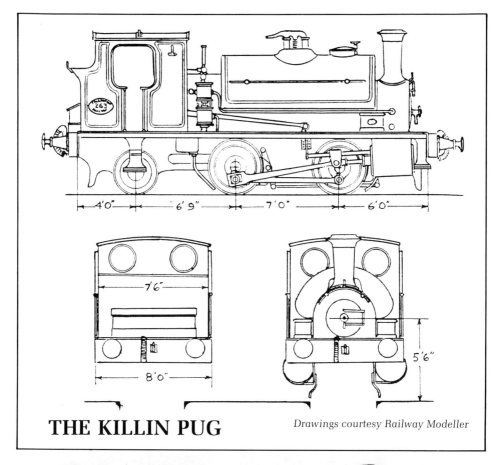

THE KILLIN PUG

Drawings courtesy Railway Modeller

This view shows one of the Killin Pugs, No. 263. This engine was re-numbered 15001 and lasted until 1947.

H.C. Casserley

coaches which connected with trains at Callander station. Anderson planned to capture this traffic.

During the early part of September 1882 he persuaded John Strain to walk with him along the route which a branch would have to take, and spy out the land. Between them the two men mapped out a suitable course for the line, which led through the property of the Earl of Moray for 6½ miles, and then for a further 2½ miles through land belonging to Lady Willoughby d'Eresby, until the Trossachs Hotel was reached near Loch Achray. Anderson knew that there might be what he called "sentimental opposition" to a railway routed through ground hallowed by association with Sir Walter Scott's verses. He planned to lessen this, firstly by keeping the line well away from the public road, and secondly by allowing sharp curvature which would reduce to a minimum the need for cuttings and embankments; this would also mean limiting the speed of the trains to a maximum of 12 mph. He favoured the use of special coaches whose roofs could be removed in good weather so that passengers could get a better view of the scenery. The line was essentially for tourist traffic and he thought that powers should be taken to close it during the off-season.

Early contacts with Mr Curr, Lady Willoughby d'Eresby's factor, and with the proprietor of the Trossachs Hotel, showed that the former was not opposed in principle to the line, while the latter, as before, received the proposal with enthusiasm and offered to contribute £4000 towards the venture. The Earl of Moray's factor, Mr Turnbull, who had been opposed to the line when it had been first suggested twelve years earlier, would not commit himself when approached again. Anderson brought his considerable powers of persuasion to bear. The line would not be an eyesore, he assured Turnbull. It might even be possible to construct it without fencing. Moreover, if the Callander and Oban did not build such a line, the North British certainly would. Turnbull seems to have left Anderson with the impression that he would recommend the idea to the Earl of Moray.

Anderson next laid his plan before the Directors of the Caledonian Railway. They replied to his letter rather cautiously. Would he make sure that all the landowners were really agreeable, and find out how much they would ask for the land? Anderson now had to visit the two factors again. Mr Turnbull proved very elusive. When at last contacted he would not give any undertaking before he had personally consulted the Earl of Moray. Finally, having done this, he gave Anderson a categorical refusal to consider the matter at all. So the scheme fell through and was never revived.

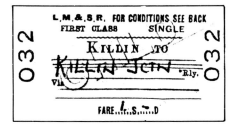

A view from the footbridge of Connel Ferry Station, looking eastwards towards Callander in April 1952.   *H.C. Casserley*

Connel Ferry Station looking westwards towards Oban. The mid-day train from Oban to Glasgow is entering, double-headed by "Black Fives" Nos. 45396 and 45488. Photographed in August 1961.   *H.B. Priestley*

Chapter Nine

The West Highland Connection and the Branch to Ballachulish

During the 1880s many schemes for new railways were proposed, and among them were some which aimed to link Inverness with Glasgow by a more westerly route than that of the Highland, taking Fort William in en route. The first of these, the Direct Inverness and Glasgow Railway, promoted in Inverness in 1881, had a short life and never reached the stage of being set out in a Parliamentary Bill. The second, for a Glasgow and North Western Railway, posed a more serious threat to the interests both of the Highland and of the Callander and Oban. It aimed to follow the eastern side of Loch Lomond, reach Crianlarich along Glen Falloch, cross the Callander and Oban here, run parallel with it as far as Tyndrum, strike north and then north-west across Rannoch Moor to the head of Glencoe, descend the latter to Loch Leven, bridge that loch at its narrowest point near its western end and then approach Fort William along the eastern side of Loch Linnhe; subsequently it would reach Inverness along the Great Glen. Had it been constructed, this line would have provided a much more direct route from Inverness to Glasgow than the existing one through Perth, and would have tapped the Callander and Oban's area between Tyndrum and Crianlarich. The Highland and Callander and Oban accordingly opposed the Bill vigorously, and were successful, though at much cost to themselves – the latter company had to spend £1000 financing its struggle and was unable to declare any dividend that half year.

They had, as it happened, scotched the snake, not killed it. In 1889 the West Highland Railway Bill came before Parliament. Though it did not include Inverness among its objectives, so that it did not conflict with the interests of the Highland, it alarmed the Directors of the Callander and Oban, whose territory was once more threatened with a line passing along Strathfillan. It was to approach Crianlarich through Helensburgh along the Gareloch, the east shore of Loch Long and the western bank of Loch Lomond, thence ascending Glen Falloch. Beyond Tyndrum it was to reach the border of Rannoch Moor near Bridge of Orchy, strike north-east and north around the eastern edges of the Moor, reaching a height of more than 1300 ft before descending to the valley of the Spean and then turning west and south-west to reach Fort William from the north-east. The whole line would resemble an irregular question-mark in shape. It was also proposed to build a branch westward to Lochailort and establish a port there to create a link with Skye and the other islands of the Outer Hebrides.

The Bill was well supported in Fort William and the Lochaber region, but the Callander and Oban viewed it with considerable alarm. The latter had already built up a considerable traffic in fish caught off the western coasts of Scotland, and the proposed new port looked like filching some of it away. Traffic might also be lost from the Strathfillan area if a quicker route to Glasgow were made possible. As a counterblast the Callander and Oban put forward a scheme of its own, for a branch down Glen Falloch to Ardlui, whence a steamer on Loch Lomond would convey passengers to Balloch, which already had a Caledonian Railway connection with Glasgow.

However, this Bill was thrown out by the Parliamentary Committee which considered it. The West Highland Bill, on the other hand, was accepted, though not the extension to Lochailort.

After this the Callander and Oban's policy was, negatively, to oppose the West Highland Bill in its passage through the Commons; positively, they declared that if that Bill were rejected they themselves would at once set in hand a line from Connel Ferry to Fort William, thus providing the sort of rail link which the people of Lochaber were seeking. In support of their case they could contend that three-quarters of that link already existed, whereas the proposed West Highland Line did not as yet exist at all; also, that their own proposed extension would pass through a populated area, whereas the West Highland route would traverse desolate and uninhabited country for much of its course, which could never generate much custom from travellers. Against them was the obvious fact that *their* line would need to cross three arms of the sea, Loch Etive, Loch Creran and Loch Leven. In the end the West Highland promoters were successful, however; their Bill became an Act and they commenced construction of their line, which was finally opened for service in August 1894.

The Callander and Oban accepted their defeat with a reasonably good grace and even persuaded themselves that the ill wind might blow them a little good. The new line crossed the older one at Crianlarich and might therefore hope to attract some custom from travellers changing there from one line to the other. With the coming of the new line this small village now enjoyed through services from both its Lower (older) and Upper (newer) stations to Glasgow. At Crianlarich the newer line crosses the older one on a high viaduct; the Upper and Lower stations were only a quarter of a mile apart, near enough to make easy interchange possible on foot. When construction began on the West Highland line in 1889 that company declared its intention of making a short spur from the north end of the Upper station which would curve steeply downwards to link up with the line to Oban half a mile west of the Lower station. The Callander and Oban agreed to this on the understanding that the West Highland bore the whole cost of construction, including the installation of signal boxes at either end of a crossing loop west of the spur. After a couple of years they became more demanding, requesting that the spur be built in such a way that it joined their own line *east* of the Lower station. This would have required some impossibly sharp curvature and the request was turned down. Then the C&O tried another tack; let a new Lower station be built at the actual junction. This too was refused. In the end the spur was built as originally arranged, as a single line veering westwards on a steep descent towards a crossing loop half a mile west of the Lower station. It was completed in October 1894.

It should now have been possible to begin through traffic, with passengers and goods from the north being able to transfer to the Callander and Oban with two reversals and have the benefit of a shorter journey to Central Scotland by way of Dunblane. But hitches occurred, in part through arguments between the two companies about how the new junction was to be operated, and in part through a quarrel with a local landowner who thought the construction of the spur had taken more of his land than he had bargained for.

The substantially built North Connel Halt, on the Ballachulish branch, looking south, with the bridge just in view.   *Lens of Sutton*

North Connel Halt (looking north) showing well the wooden platform and support timbers.   *Real Photographs*

The approach to Connel Ferry bridge, from the north, photographed in August 1961 showing the small keeper's hut.   *H.B. Priestley*

The approach to Connel Ferry bridge from the south, photographed in 1952. A gate bars road vehicles from entering while the train crosses.   *H.C. Casserley*

The consequence was that for three seasons cattle sent from Lochaber to markets in Perth had to travel an extra 65 miles, going round by way of Glasgow, to the great annoyance of their despatchers since the charges for conveyance were so much greater. Not until midwinter in 1897 was the junction at last opened.

A further disappointment now awaited the people of Oban. It was natural for them to think that they would now be able to enjoy through travel to Glasgow by a route 20 miles shorter (and therefore cheaper) than that through Callander and Stirling – or that at the very least convenient connections could be arranged. The Callander and Oban, however, did not see why they should oblige their customers by making such arrangements. It was always possible, of course, for a passenger for Glasgow to book to Crianlarich, walk between the two stations and then re-book, but anyone doing this had usually to face a long wait; he might save money, but not time. This state of affairs went on and on. Even when British Railways assumed control of both lines in 1948 and the question of one line benefiting at the other's expense no longer applied, it was the same. Occasional excursion trains were to use the spur, but no regular services. Nature settled the matter in 1965 by causing a landslide near Lochearnhead, after which the older line was closed between Callander and Crianlarich and all traffic from Oban was routed to Glasgow over the spur.

In 1896 two other branch proposals were made. Inveraray, the small county town of Argyllshire, had been left on one side when the Callander and Oban and the West Highland were opening up the country to the north of it. Its inhabitants were dependent on road transport – a two-hours' coach journey to connect with the train at Dalmally – or had to use the steamers which called at the pier on Loch Fyne. The Callander and Oban proposed to make a branch from Dalmally which would climb to a 600 ft summit two miles beyond the village of Cladich and descend Glen Aray to the town itself. The West Highland countered this by proposing a branch from Arrochar which would parallel the existing coach road up Glen Croe, across the Rest-and-be-Thankful pass and down Glen Kinglas to the shore of Loch Fyne at St. Catherine's, whence a ferry would transfer passengers to the town. The latter route promised a shorter journey to Glasgow, but at the expense of a water crossing, and it would have been a more considerable undertaking than the Callander and Oban's scheme since it would have involved some very heavy gradients. It had the advantage of being acceptable to the Duke of Argyll, who owned Inveraray Castle and felt like Wordsworth had done about intrusive railways. The Callander and Oban, for its part, was prepared to excavate a quite unnecessary tunnel so that their line should not offend the ducal eyes. Of the two schemes, Parliament finally approved the West Highland's, but that company never built the line, and probably saved themselves a great deal of money in consequence. Inveraray remained the pleasant and somnolent backwater that it still is. No vessels now come to the pier and one can only reach the town by road, a twice-daily bus being available for non-motorists.

The railway-less Great Glen between Fort William and Inverness beckoned would-be railway promoters invitingly even after the failure of the Glasgow and North Western project. The West Highland, once it had reached Fort William, indicated that it had it in mind to build a branch from Spean Bridge to Inverness, which would have been some 50 miles long and not steeply graded, following a natural route that nowhere rose more than 150 ft above sea level. The Highland met this threat to invade its own territory by promoting a branch of its own to Fort William. In 1894 the Callander and Oban had determined that they were going to build a line to Inverness, branching from their own line at Connel Ferry, and had commissioned an eminent civil engineer to survey the route. The initial estimate was that it would cost something like a million pounds, a figure which alone would have seemed enough to prevent them from going further with the project. By now the West Highland and Highland companies had given up their intentions to invade the Great Glen, but they still viewed the C & O's scheme with disfavour. Their opposition was enough to deter the latter from going ahead with the full scheme, but the construction of the line as far as Ballachulish was approved, and part of what had been promised as an alternative to the West Highland line now became a possibility. The Highland Railway was indifferent to what might happen south of Loch Leven; the West Highland were opposed to their competitor approaching so far towards Lochaber. So two Bills were prepared to be put before Parliament, one for a branch to Ballachulish from Connel, the other for an extension of the West Highland southwards to the same place, crossing the narrowest part of Loch Leven by a bridge that would open to admit shipping. Ballachulish, being the site of a large slate quarry, promised lucrative traffic.

However, the West Highland ran into opposition from the people of Fort William for the same reason as the Callander and Oban had fallen foul of many of the people of Oban in 1879; an extension of their existing line would spoil their waterfront and deter visitors. The slate quarry owners, too, were not happy with the bridge proposal, fearing it might interfere with the free movement of the steamers that came for cargoes of slates. Both companies carried their cases to Parliament. Each had its scheme approved. But the West Highland found that in effect it had lost the day, because the scheme for the Loch Leven bridge was turned down at the same time, and a line that could not reach the quarries would be useless. The Callander and Oban was therefore left in possession of the field.

The branch when built was nearly 28 miles long, diverging to the north a little beyond Connel Ferry station and ending half a mile east of the Ballachulish Hotel, with a branch to the slate quarries. It was at first intended that trains should run through from Oban without having to reverse at Connel, and the construction of a spur line was begun to enable this. But there were obvious disadvantages from the point of view of a traveller from the south or east, who would have to travel through to Oban to board such trains, and the company changed its mind when the spur had been partly completed. All trains were to run into Connel from Oban and most would connect there with trains from Callander, and vice versa. Construction began in September 1898, the contractor being John Best, who had been responsible for completing the Killin Branch.

[59 & 60 Vict.] *Callander and Oban Railway Act,* 1896. [**Ch. cxci.**]

CHAPTER cxci.

An Act to empower the Callander and Oban Railway Company to extend their Railway from Connel Ferry to Ballachulish and for other purposes. [7th August 1896.] A.D. 1896.

WHEREAS an extension of the Callander and Oban Railway from near Connel Ferry to Ballachulish would be of local and public advantage and it is expedient for that purpose that the Callander and Oban Railway Company (herein-after called " the Company ") should be authorised to construct the railways herein-after described and that the powers of this Act should be conferred on them in reference thereto :

And whereas the existing railways and works of the Company are maintained and worked in perpetuity by the Caledonian Railway Company in pursuance of certain agreements between those Companies confirmed or given effect to by the Callander and Oban Railway Act 1865 and the Callander and Oban Railway (Abandonment &c.) Act 1870 and it is expedient that the provisions of those agreements should be extended and made applicable to the railways by this Act authorised and to the maintenance and working thereof by the Caledonian Railway Company : 28 & 29 Vict. c. cclxvi. 33 Vict. c. ix.

And whereas it is expedient that the Company should be authorised to raise additional capital for the purposes of this Act and to pay interest out of capital during the construction of the works authorised by this Act :

And whereas under the authority of the Acts relating to the undertaking of the Company the Caledonian Railway Company at present hold shares or stock in such undertaking of the following amounts viz. two hundred and thirty-three thousand eight hundred pounds of preference shares or stock and one hundred and eighty-two thousand six hundred pounds of ordinary shares or stock and it is expedient that they should be authorised to subscribe further capital to the undertaking of the Company in manner herein-after provided :

And whereas plans and sections showing the lines and levels of the several railways authorised by this Act and also a book of

[*Price* 1s. 9d.]   A   1

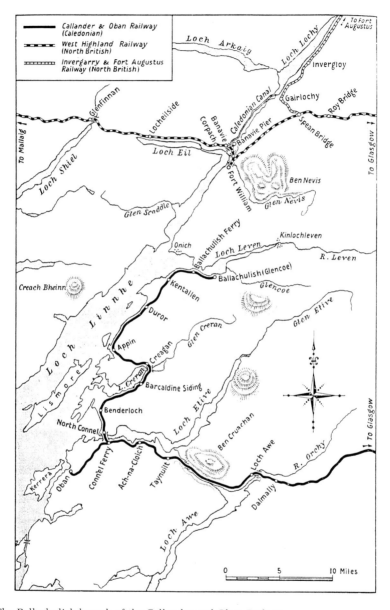

The Ballachulish branch of the Callander and Oban Railway.

Courtesy, *Railway Magazine*

Connel rail bus with car-carrying wagon in tow.   *Courtesy, David and Charles*

Creagan bridge on the Ballachulish branch.   *Courtesy, David and Charles*

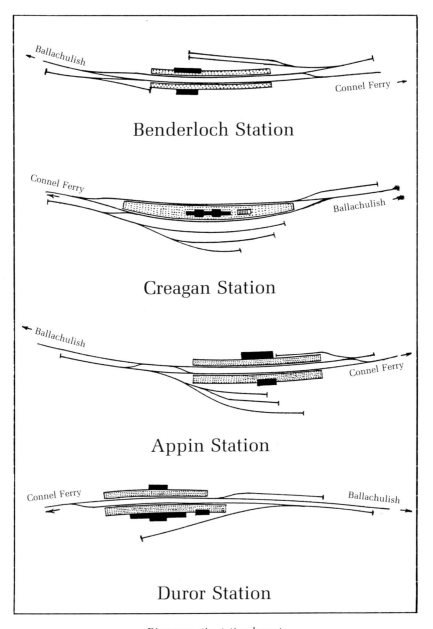

Benderloch Station

Creagan Station

Appin Station

Duror Station

Diagrammatic station layouts

The magnificent Connel Ferry Bridge seen in 1934.   E. R. Morten

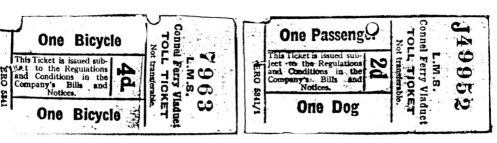

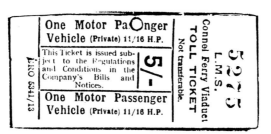

Benderloch Station, looking towards Oban in April 1952.   *H.C. Casserley*

Benderloch Station, but this time looking towards Ballachulish.   *Lens of Sutton*

Barcaldine Halt, on the Ballachulish branch north of Benderloch, a somewhat Heath Robinson style of construction. *Real Photographs*

The island platform at Creagan, looking towards Ballachulish. The Station building's style is again different from others on the branch. *Real Photographs*

Creagan Station, looking south. The branch line passenger train is crossing with a southbound goods train (on the left) taken in August 1961. Note the subway to the other platform and exit. *H.B. Priestley*

Two branch line trains cross at Appin Station in January 1962. The engine facing the camera is an unusual visitor, a Class 4 ex-L.M.S. 2-6-4 tank No. 46448 on the 12.26 pm Ballachulish to Oban, whilst the train crews are exchanging tablets. The other train is hauled by No. 55233. *H.B. Priestley*

Photographed from the Ballachulish to Oban train (hauled by No. 55233) just as it enters Appin Station. The engine on the right is No. 57441, a Drummond 0−6−0 still active in January 1962 when this view was captured.   *H.B. Priestley*

Appin Station looking towards Ballachulish. Note the Station shelter and signal box on the left.   *Real Photographs*

Duror Station looking in a sorry state after the removal of the crossing loop.
Real Photographs

Kentallen Station looking towards Oban. The 10.48 am from Ballachulish hauled by No. 55233 is about to cross with Class 4 No. 46468, with the 8.25 an ex-Oban service in August 1961. *H.B. Priestley*

Kentallen Station, looking towards Oban. This view shows the rather substantial buildings provided at the station. *Lens of Sutton*

Kentallen Station looking towards Ballachulish. A down passenger train is crossing with an up goods behind Drummond 0–6–0 No. 57441; August 1961. Note the water column and lattice post signal. *H.B. Priestley*

A view of the curved platform of the quaint Ballachulish Ferry Halt; probably taken during the 'Fifties.   *Lens of Sutton*

Ballachulish Ferry Halt: a later picture after the cutting back of shrubs and foliage, and probably photographed not long before closure. Even as a Halt, it had a clock, toilets and waiting rooms.   *Lens of Sutton*

The end of the branch; Ballachulish Station. This view photographed in April 1952 shows the station forecourt and the goods shed. H.C. Casserley

Ballachulish Station with the 10.48 am (hauled by No. 55233) about to leave for Oban in June 1961. *H.B. Priestley*

Opposite: A fine aerial view of Ballachulish Station area taken in 1936 from the hills.
It shows the station (*top left*), goods shed (*centre top*) and engine shed (*right top*). Note
the narrow gauge railway in the centre carrying slates to the yard.   *R.W. Kidner*

Looking towards the buffer stops at Ballachulish Station in April 1952. Note the slate
quarry where the previous photograph was taken in 1936.   *H.C. Casserley*

Ballachulish sidings, turntable, and engine shed with No. 55196 beside water tank.
        H.C. Casserley

Train for Oban taking water at Ballachulish alongside the signal box with 0−4−4 tank No. 55233 in charge. *Lens of Sutton*

Ballachulish Station showing the release loop points photographed from the buffer-stops. *Lens of Sutton*

The route originally proposed would have run closer to Loch Linnhe, aiming from Benderloch somewhat to the west of north towards the island of Eriska, then crossing the mouth of Loch Creran, passing close to Port Appin, swinging round the head of the sea inlet of Loch Laich, and then following the shore as far as the outflow of the river Duror. Finally it cut across the base of the Ardsheal peninsula and so through Kentallen to Ballachulish. A last-minute change of plan took the line further to the east, to cross Loch Creran at its narrowest point; this denied Port Appin a convenient railway station – the actual one to bear the name Appin was to be 3 miles away. The alteration increased the length of the line, but had the advantage of not requiring two bridges, one of considerable length, on to and across from Eriska Island.

Changes were also made in the sitings of intermediate stations. At first the intention had been to place them at Ledaig, Creagan Ferry (on the southern side of Loch Creran), Portnacroish, Cuil (near the mouth of the Duror), Ardsheal and Ballachulish Ferry; at Cuil and Ardsheal there were to be piers serving steamers on Loch Linnhe. In the event the stations were sited at Benderloch (just below the pre-historic hill-fort of Beregonium, ½ mile north of Ledaig), Creagan (on the northern bank of Loch Creran), Portnacroish (re-named Appin), Cuil (re-named Duror, a good 1½ miles from that village) and Kentallen (1 mile beyond the intended site of Ardsheal station). Neither at Cuil nor at Ardsheal was any pier built.

The finished branch was seven times longer than that to Killin. It had no gradients to speak of, and for most of its length it was close beside Loch Linnhe or its bays and inlets. If one wished for views it was best to sit on the seaward side of the train. After crossing Connel Bridge (fully described in Appendix One) from which one could get a brief glimpse of Loch Etive to the right between its girders, the line ran close to the waterside of Ardmucknish Bay, giving views of the wooded promontory of Garbh Ard, the south end of Lismore island and the hills of Morven and Eastern Mull. At Benderloch the line swung away to the north-east across the neck of a peninsula, to reach the water's edge again near Barcaldine and follow it for some four miles. The views to the left were of the Appin peninsula and the hills beyond, across Loch Creran. At South Creagan the line swerved inland and curved to the left on an embankment, to cross over the loch by Creagan Bridge (Appendix One) at the point where its width is constricted to a few hundred feet. The road from Oban to Ballachulish passes beneath the railway under the single southern arch of the masonry approach. As one crossed the bridge there were fine views on both sides over the waters of the loch; the line then entered a short cutting and after emerging crossed the road once more. The latter had had to make a detour of 5 miles while the train required less than ½ mile between the two points where it crossed it.

Beyond Creagan station the route followed the north shore of the loch westwards for a mile or so, and to the left one could see across the water to where one had been travelling a few minutes earlier. Then the loch's shore trends away to the south-west and both line and road cut across the neck of the Appin peninsula, through woods and fields. After 2½ miles salt water was reached once more at Loch Laich, a tidal inlet with a small islet upon which the eye-catching Castle Stalker perches. Here was Appin station, named after the area, the adjacent village being Portnacroish. The line then turned round to the north-east again, following the shore, and kept between the road and the water's edge for some 7 miles, with pleasant views across Loch Linnhe, with the islands of Shuna and Balnagowan prominent in the foreground. In the decade before World War I there was always plenty of shipping to be seen on the loch, going to or coming from the Caledonian Canal, which was used much more then for through traffic to the North Sea than it is now.

Eventually Duror station was reached, and another intrusion of land, the Ardsheal peninsula, blocked the seaward view for a while, as the line struck inland up the valley of the river Duror and aimed for the saddle between the hill of Ardsheal and the huge bulk of Ben Vair to the east. Crossing the low summit one descended to Kentallen station (now converted to a restaurant with a magnificent view of Loch Linnhe from its dining-room) and followed the shore again as far as the entrance of Loch Leven. Quite close to the line, though not actually visible from it, was a monument commemorating one of the more unpleasant episodes of Highland history. On this spot James of the Glen, a prominent inhabitant of Appin and a Jacobite sympathiser, was hanged for a crime he certainly did not commit, the murder of the Duke of Argyll's factor in an ambush a little further to the south; the affair is fictionally recorded in Robert Louis Stevenson's novel *Kidnapped*. To the left the view from the train was of the wooded banks of the northern shore at the entrance to Loch Leven, which narrows to a gap not much wider than the strait where the line crossed Loch Creran; here there was a vehicle ferry and close to the latter was the single-platform halt of Ballachulish Ferry. A further two miles and the terminus was reached at Ballachulish village. Here before World War I there were connections with a steamer which took one to the head of Loch Leven; this was the village of Kinlochleven's only contact with the outside world unless one walked or rode. During that war German prisoners were given the task of building a road from Glencoe to Kinlochleven; once this was finished and in use the steamer service became less patronised and was eventually discontinued.

Connel Ferry Station with "Black Fives" Nos. 45396 and 45488 double-heading the mid-day train from Oban to Glasgow in August 1961.   *H.B. Priestley*

Chapter Ten

Locomotives and Rolling Stock: 1880–1965

It had been the Caledonian Railway's intention to use tank engines for all traffic on the Callander and Oban line once the extension to Oban was finished, and certain locomotives were earmarked for use. Fifteen 2–4–2s, with 5 ft 8 in. coupled wheels and radial axleboxes in front and rear, had already been designed by George Brittain, locomotive superintendent on the Caledonian until his retirement through ill-health in 1882, and these came into use at once. Their principal dimensions and characteristics are noted in the table at the end of this chapter, together with those of other locomotive types which followed them. They were neat little engines, with outside cylinders and tall stove-pipe chimneys of the type favoured by Brittain and his predecessor Banjamin Conner. However, they proved to be quite unsatisfactory. They rode roughly at speed, regularly ran hot, and had great difficulty in staying on the road since their front and rear axleboxes were not radially true. The tendency to leave the rails was so marked that special re-railing equipment had to be carried in the guard's van of each train hauled by one of them, so that it could be put back quickly on to the track. In consequence there was a great deal of late running and John Anderson was quick to lodge complaints.

The Caledonian's first idea was to borrow from the London and North Western one of Francis Webb's similar 2–4–2 tank engines, intending to purchase some if the loaned engine proved satisfactory. Trials with one were duly carried out, but evidently its performance was not impressive as it was returned. It was instead decided to design an engine of a different type. The faulty 2–4–2s were transferred to other branch lines after having their front axleboxes modified; this, however, did not cure their propensity for derailment. Scrapping began in 1900 and twelve years later all but one had disappeared.

After this inauspicious beginning the Caledonian sent nine tender locomotives as a stopgap measure. They were 0–4–2s which Benjamin Conner had built in 1878, and had short 4-wheel tenders so that they could be turned on the small turntables which the C &O possessed. They had been built as goods engines, but their 5 ft 2 in. driving wheels were no disadvantage on a heavily-graded line. They took over from the radial tanks in May 1881 and for a year or so had the line to themselves. They were rather peculiar in appearance, not only for their curved footplating and overhanging cylinders, but also for having a sandbox built on to each driving-wheel splasher, forwards in the case of the front drivers, rearwards over those behind them. This was almost but not quite a unique arrangement; it had been used on one much earlier engine in 1865. These 0–4–2s remained on the Oban line for several years, though their monopoly of the passenger services ended when their destined successors, Brittain's "Oban Bogies", began to make their appearance

These latter engines, designed by Brittain just before his retirement in 1882, and built by Dübs and Company, of Govan, Glasgow, came out in the same year in a batch of ten. They were very like David Jones' "Skye Bogies" which were being built for the Highland Railway at the same time, for use on a very similar railway, the Dingwall and Kyle of Lochalsh line, so it is

0−6−0 "Jumbo" No. 17424, taken at Callander not long after the 1923 grouping.
Real Photographs

A fine detail study of the Oban Bogie "Mark I" No. 183 (Caledonian number).
Real Photographs

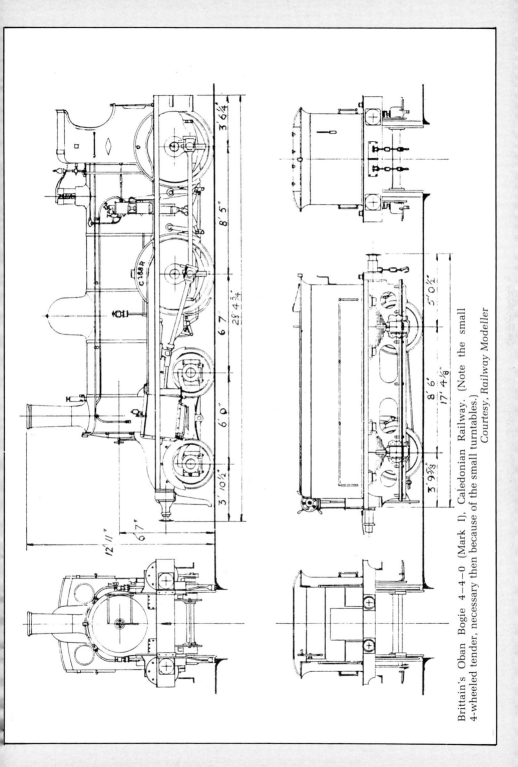

Britain's Oban Bogie 4–4–0 (Mark I), Caledonian Railway. (Note the small 4-wheeled tender, necessary then because of the small turntables.)

Courtesy, Railway Modeller

Oban Bogie "Mark I" No. 1181 outside Oban engine shed in March 1921.
L.C.G.B., Ken Nunn Collection

An 0−4−4 tank No. 192 in original condition as built by Drummond. Note the solid spokeless rear bogie wheels. *L.C.G.B., Ken Nunn Collection*

Oban Bogie "Mark II", 4–6–0, No. 14606 (originally Caledonian No. 52) heading the mid-day train from Oban to Glasgow in the middle 'Twenties.

L.C.G.B., Ken Nunn Collection

Special train from Glasgow with railway officials seen here approaching Oban in June 1925 behind a rebuilt "Jumbo" (travelling tender first). *L.C.G.B., Ken Nunn Collection*

0–6–0 "Jumbo" No. 17423 at Oban on pilot duty.   *Real Photographs*

4–6–0 Oban Bogie "Mark III", 4–6–0 No. 14652 at Oban shed in July 1931.
H.C. Casserley

Portrait of a Caledonian Railway '55' class 4–6–0 Oban Bogie "Mark II" No. 14607 at Oban in June 1927.   *H.C. Casserley*

Oban Bogie "Mark III" No. 14623 at head of train entering Oban in September 1933.
                                                                    E.R. Morton

possible that the two men collaborated. They were 4–4–0s with front ends greatly resembling those of the locomotives built by Alexander Allan, a former locomotive superintendent of the London and North Western Railway. The outside cylinders were steeply inclined and their upper parts appeared to be, so to speak, surfacing through the running plate. As compared with the "Skye Bogies", their cylinders were the same in size, their coupled wheels were only an inch less in diameter, 5 ft 2 in., and their boiler pressure was 130 lb. to the square inch as compared with the 140 lb. of the Highland engines; the weights of the two types were about the same. The Caledonian engines differed in having a splasher over each bogie wheel, stovepipe chimneys and short four-wheeled tenders like their predecessors.

The first-generation "Oban Bogies" were very popular with their drivers and had no difficulty in keeping time until train loads increased at the end of the century. They coped well with the line's fierce gradients on either side of the three summits at Glenoglehead, Tyndrum and Glencruitten. To augment their hauling capacity John McIntosh, who became locomotive superintendent after Brittain's successors, Lambie and Drummond, had both left the scene, rebuilt all ten of them between 1898 and 1901 with larger fireboxes and a higher boiler pressure of 150 lb. to the square inch. He also gave them larger six-wheel tenders since the C &O turntables had now been enlarged and were able to take them. These locomotives had comparatively long lives; not until 1922 were the first two withdrawn; the last two to go were scrapped eight years later.

Dugald Drummond's particular contribution to the Callander and Oban line was the designing of two little tank locomotives for the Killin branch. These were 0–4–2 saddle tanks with driving wheels 3 ft 8 in. in diameter and trailing wheels only 2 ft 6 in. across. Their storage capacities were on the same scale: the tank held only 800 gallons of water and a mere ¾ ton of coal, though side rails were later added to the bunker which allowed an extra half-ton to be loaded. On a line less than six miles long such deficiencies scarcely mattered. What did matter was their braking ability. The Board of Trade had insisted, as a condition of their approving the branch, that locomotives and coaches should all have Westinghouse air brakes fitted, and this was done. The safety valves were on the top of the dome, in true Drummond style, the dome itself being embedded in the saddle-tank with only its top showing. The long chimneys were of the built-up variety (Drummond detested stovepipes) and the cylinders were outside the frames. Each engine weighed just under 34¼ tons. They worked the Killin branch until 1895, and lasted elsewhere on the Caledonian system long enough eventually to receive LMS numbers.

Drummond's celebrated 0–6–0 "Jumbos" were also used on the C &O, not only for freight traffic but occasionally as pilots for passenger trains, or even working passenger trains in pairs. They were found all over the Caledonian railway, working freight trains, and were extremely versatile. Together with similar engines, basically of the same design but with modifications, they came to number 244, 83 of which were constructed in Drummond's time. All lasted long enough to be included in LMS stock and received appropriate five-figure numbering.

John MacIntosh, as mentioned above, rebuilt Brittain's "Oban Bogies", but also designed larger locomotives as traffic on the line increased and trains got heavier. In 1902 he brought out a "second generation" "Oban Bogie", in a batch of five, four more following three years later. They looked very different from the engines they supplanted. The boilers were longer, they had inside cylinders, and they were six-coupled. There was some doubt as to whether they would negotiate the curves on the line, but in practice they had no trouble doing this, and were very well-liked by their drivers. In order to obtain as short a coupled wheelbase as possible the front and middle coupled wheels' rims almost touched one another. The longer boiler – 14 ft against 10 ft – and cylinders half as large again as those of the 4–4–0s, with a steam pressure of 175 lb. to the square inch, resulted in a striking increase of power. Their tractive effort was higher than that of any other locomotive in the country at the time when the first batch appeared, excepting only that of the Great Western "Saint" class which appeared at the same time. They were fitted with tablet-exchange apparatus to allow tokens to be exchanged without stopping. They were sleek and handsome engines and great favourites with their crews.

So much for the principal types to which the haulage of the chief passenger trains was entrusted during the period of the Callander and Oban's existence as an independent company. One other type needs a mention – the 0–4–4 tank engine, first built by Dugald Drummond in the mid-eighties and then developed and modified by his successors Lambie and MacIntosh. They eventually replaced Drumond's little "pugs" on the Killin branch, and were subsequently used elsewhere on the C &O, almost monopolizing the Ballachulish branch right up until its closure. This branch became, as it were, the final pasture for ageing 0–4–4s as the lines on which they had previously operated were closed one by one in LMS and early BR days. Drummond's first batch with this wheel arrangement had 5 ft driving wheels and solid unspoked bogie wheels only 2 ft 6 in. in diameter. Lambie's and MacIntosh's modified versions increased the sizes to 5 ft 9 in. and 3 ft 2 in., the latter being of the conventional spoked type. When some of the former were first put on the Ballachulish run they had cow-catchers fitted, but these were soon found to be unnecessary. However, the line ran close to the public road for the greater part of its length, and the noise the engines made sometimes frightened the horses. The local authority lodged complaints and threatened to report the matter to the Board of Trade. If it did so, the latter seems to have taken no notice. These locomotives had quite long lives; even some of Drummond's lasted long enough to be absorbed into LMS stock without having been re-built, and one of MacIntosh's, built in 1895, was not withdrawn until 1961. They were sprightly little engines, able to accelerate quickly to 55 mph on open stretches of the line.

One single, unique vehicle deserves mention; though not a steam loco-motive, it certainly ran upon rails under its own power and was used for passenger traffic. This was the "Connel Bus", a motor vehicle with a 30 hp petrol engine and seats for 23 people as well as the driver. It began to operate in July 1909, purely to carry passengers across the Connel Ferry bridge to North Connel in between regular train services. Originally a road vehicle

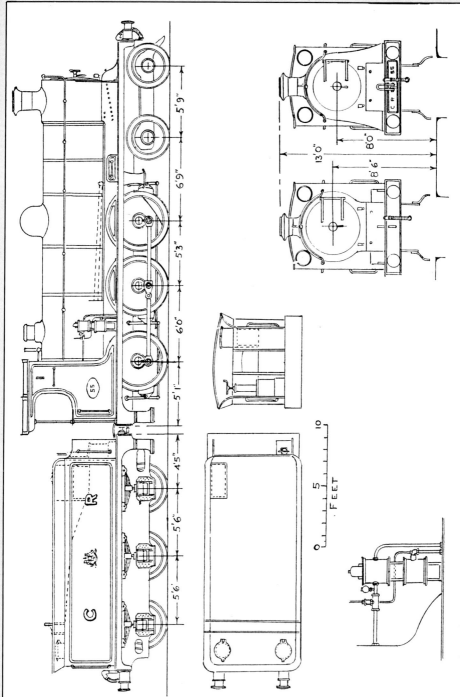

McIntosh's Oban Bogie 4–6–0 (Mark II): Caledonian Railway. Drawn by W. Hardin-Osborne.

Courtesy Railway Modeller

A freight train for Oban standing at Killin Junction, headed by diesel locomotives
Nos. D 6119 and D 6109 in June 1963.   *H.C. Casserley*

A Drummond "Jumbo", piloting an ex-Highland Railway "Clan", entering Dalmally
Station, September 1934 on a train for Oban.   *E.R. Morten*

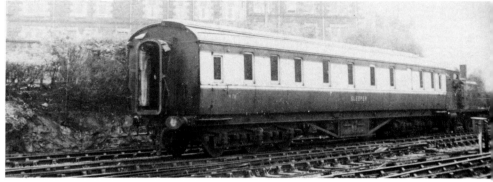

68 foot composite 1st and 3rd class sleeper coach at Oban, after being detached from the night train from Euston in April 1952.   *H.C. Casserley*

Third class brake carriage, built at St Rollox Works in 1919, for the Caledonian Railway, standing at Oban in April 1952.   *H.C. Casserley*

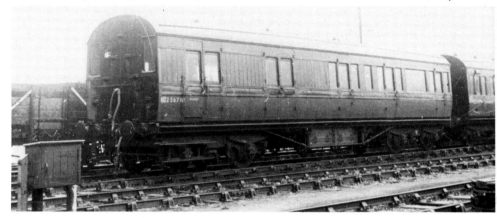

Ex-N.B.R. coach No. DE 32029, built at Cowlairs in 1909, converted in 1953 to a dormitory vehicle for British Rail staff, standing at Loch Tay in 1957.   *H.C. Casserley*

used in the suburbs of Glasgow, it was bought by the Caledonian which adapted the wheels to take flanged tyres and run on rails. It was taken under its own power all the way from St Rollox Works to Connel. Having arrived there, it was adapted also to haul a wagon so that a car could be taken across behind the passengers. In this way a roundabout journey of some 90 miles by way of Tyndrum and Glencoe could be replaced by a mere half-mile journey over the bridge. This pair of vehicles continued to trundle at intervals between Connel Ferry and North Connel until World War I.

Towards the end of the separate existences of the Caledonian and Callander and Oban the former's locomotive superintendent, MacIntosh's successor William Pickersgill, decided that the latter needed engines of greater power. He designed eight 4–6–0s, six of which were drafted on to it. In appearance these looked larger than MacIntosh's second generation of "Oban Bogies" and should have been an improvement on them. In fact they were not, and the reasons for this are somewhat obscure.

The new "191 Class" came out in December 1922, in time to receive the Caledonian blue livery before that railway was swallowed up by the London, Midland and Scottish system (the merger did not occur, in the Caledonian's case, before July 1923) and were, like other Pickersgill types, three-cylindered engines with outside Walschaerts valve gear. Surprisingly, they had slide valves instead of piston valves; even more surprisingly, they were not superheated. They were handsome to look at, and having shorter chimneys and domes than their predecessors they looked more powerful than they really were. In fact their boilers were higher-pitched than those of the MacIntosh locomotives, so as to clear the larger coupled wheels. Their cylinder capacity was half as large again as that of the engines they were meant to replace, but their boilers were almost the same size, with a pressure only ten pounds greater, and the total heating surface was slightly less. One wonders, therefore, if their poor performance was not due in part, at any rate, to their being over-cylindered. The derived valve-gear for the inside cylinder, too, did not function well, and valve-spindles were always breaking. The drivers on the Oban road complained that they were sluggish engines. Consequently, as soon as the Caledonian had been absorbed in the LMS, the latter's locomotive department began to look around for a more satisfactory engine. They found it on the old Highland Railway's recently-designed "Clan" class which Mr Christopher Cumming had built for use on the Perth-Inverness main line.

The "Clans", four of which appeared in 1919 and four more in 1921, were the most powerful locomotives that the Highland had built (apart from the celebrated and notorious "Rivers" which because of their supposed over-weight and oversize had resulted in the summary dismissal of their designer, Cumming's predecessor, and their own sale to the Caledonian, on which system they were used for goods train haulage). The "Clan" 4–6–0 had two outside cylinders, Walschaerts valve gear working piston valves, large boilers and a greater heating area than the "191 Class", and were superheated. A raised running-plate on either side which extended from the smokebox to the cab and was covered in at the side carried the locomotive's name; the splashers that covered the tops of the driving wheels were only just visible. The front view resembled that of a London, Brighton and South Coast engine, though Cumming had had no connection with that railway; it was probably mere coincidence. The "Clans" could undoubtedly pull, despite the fact that their driving wheels were larger even than those of the Pickersgill engines. O.S. Nock, in his book on the Highland Railway, mentions an experience he had when footplate-travelling on the Callander and Oban line in the 'thirties:

> I shall always remember a trip I was privileged to make on the footplate of the 5.15 pm express up from Oban, when for a load of 375 tons we had one of those puny Pickersgill non-superheater 4–6–0s as pilot to *Clan MacKinnon*. I rode on the pilot engine for part of the way and watched her gradually drop pressure and put up a characteristically feeble show. Behind us the "Clan" was roaring her heart out, taking fully three-quarters of the load, if not more, and our fireman kept pointing enviously to her safety valves. Despite the sustained thrashing on banks like that from Dalmally up Glen Lochy the white feather was always showing on *Clan MacKinnon*.

Towards the end of the 'thirties, however, a new type of locomotive began to take over from the "Clans", and soon came to be in charge of all traffic, both passenger and goods, on the main line. This was Stanier's class five mixed traffic 4–6–0, the celebrated "Black Five", arguably that designer's most successful locomotive and certainly more widely distributed over the LMS system than any other locomotive had ever been, from Dorset to Caithness. Probably no other locomotive type was ever built in this country in such large numbers. Between April 1934 and October 1947 no fewer than 842 were ordered, the last 80 appearing new from Horwich and Crewe works after the parent company had been absorbed into British Railways. Its design formed the basis of one of British Railways' standard steam types, the class 5MT 4–6–0, of which 172 were built between 1951 and 1957. The original design had many variants (though none of the more unusual ones ever appeared on the Oban line). Some had Caprotti valve gear and external steam pipes that were much enlarged and not at all pretty; some had the top-feed apparatus in a container which looked like a steam dome but was not one; some had Timken roller bearings on their axleboxes; a few even bore names. But all were painted black and all had the same nominal tractive effort. All, too, had parts of their framing cut away in front so that they could be used on as many parts of the LMS system as possible and have the necessary clearances of lineside structures and platform edges.

The "Black Fives" began to work on the Oban line in November 1938 and stayed till the end of steam. After World War II no other type was seen on its main route until the diesels began to take over; the "Clans" and Pickersgill locomotives had now all gone for scrap. The deep sound of the "Black Fives" hooters was unmistakable as it echoed along the glens. When the writer first came to live in Strathfillan, at Crianlarich and close to the point where the spur from the West Highland joins the Callander and Oban and where trains passed one another on the crossing loop, two of them regularly waited at the bottom of our garden at about ten o'clock every weekday morning, each with a few trucks and vans, shunted and waiting for the 8 am from Glasgow to pass. Every so often one would let off steam with a terrifying noise which sent the cat racing indoors, and any washing which might have been hung out to dry would be sprinkled with smuts from the two chimneys if the wind was from the north. We soon learned to time our clothes-drying accordingly.

Information about the passenger rolling stock used on the Callander and Oban is rather scanty. All one can say now about the earliest years is that the Caledonian sent to the line such vehicles as they felt they could spare. Photographs taken at about the time when the line was opened show four-wheeled vehicles with flattish roofs from which cylindrical covers pro-truded upwards, covering the oil lamps beneath. Another photograph, of an excursion train from Falkirk to Dalmally, which became derailed near the latter station, shows that similar coaches were still being used in 1886, though the oil lamp covers had now given place to roof ventilators. These narrow, straight-sided carriages could have been neither roomy nor com-fortable. In 1889, complete sets of three coaches were put into service; each set consisted of a first class carriage with a brake third at either end, and took 150 passengers at most. Each vehicle was 45 ft long and ran on two four-wheel bogies. The first class vehicles had four compartments along the centre of each vehicle; next to the outer two of these were toilet com-partments communicating with them; also communicating, and at the end of each coach, were two coupé compartments. The third class vehicles were much less luxurious, packing over twice as many people into only one-and-a-half times the space, and without benefit of toilets. Lighting was by gas. A journey in one of the coupés, in its later days when the carriage had been relegated to the Ballachulish branch, is described by Mr G.W.J. Potter in the *Railway Magazine* for September 1912. The glass-windowed ends of the coaches made it:

> . . possible for the passenger to see the end of the coach in front or behind. Should there be no other coach in front the engine is visible, and in either case a greatly-increased angle of view is obtained over the country on each side of the track. One day the passenger accommodation was somewhat limited in the Ballachulish train, and before leaving Connel Ferry two elderly ladies decided to travel – but with evident misgivings – in a coupé which was otherwise unoccupied. This was next to the train engine, one of the smaller tanks, running bunker-first. Away we went, and the journey to North Connel must upon the whole have been all right; but upon reaching Benderloch, our second stop, the ladies had apparently had more than enough of this type of railway travelling. They hurried out of the com-partment directly the train stopped, and with ejaculations of "It was dreadful" and "I could not bear any more", sought refuge in another carriage.

Presumably the fugitives did not like the appearance of the locomotive's front end – it was probably an 0–4–4 tank – or the sound of its exhaust; anyhow, the writer and his companion took their places, and,

> the remainder of the journey in that coupé was nevertheless a thing to be remembered by us. The line runs by the sea for many a mile, and the views are charming. Locomotive interest was also to the fore, as a considerable part of the work on the footplate could be watched with ease and comfort.

In 1910 some 8-wheeled semi-corridor coaches were made for use on the Oban line, and rather later some ex-LNW West Coast Joint Stock vehicles supplemented them. In 1914 the ultimate in first class travel comfort appeared for a few months; the *Maid of Morven*, a Pullman observation car with lounge accommodation and a kitchen buffet which, being at the end of a vestibuled train, could also serve meals and refreshments to other passengers in seats in the adjoining vehicle. The décor was luxurious. Mr John Thomas, in his history of this line, describes the interior as follows:

> The internal decoration, after the Sheraton period, was lavish. The walls were panelled in finely-figured pearwood, and there were marquetry pilasters with details after Pergolesi. The Bergère chairs were upholstered in brown tapestry with a floral trellis design. The light brackets were of chased metal, and table-lamps with hand-painted silk shades were provided. A heavy pile plain brown carpet covered the floor.

This was the first observation car to have been built in Great Britain. The acme of Edwardian travelling luxury, it was re-introduced on the Oban line in March 1919 and continued to run until 1929, by which time patronage was falling off. The charge for use by passengers, over and above the first class fare, was half a crown (the equivalent of several pounds of our money).

Pullman dining cars were also used on other trains on the Oban line contemporaneously with the *Maid*, and these too had sumptuous interiors. They were also available to third class passengers, though only while they were taking meals. The thing to do, it seems, was to use it on the early train from Glasgow when breakfast was served; there were not likely to be many users at that time, so that one could obtain second helpings of every thing and as much coffee as one wished; the food had been prepared and there was no point in wasting it. '

Once the Callander and Oban had come under LMS ownership coaches from other parts of that system began to supplement and eventually replace the former vehicles; complete corridor trains took the place of the former non-corridor stock and after a while ordinary restaurant cars replaced the Pullmans. Eventually the 57 ft-long standard LMS coaches built during the thirties appeared, and third class travel then became very rewarding, as the writer discovered during a brief visit to Argyllshire in the early 'forties when he used the Oban line for the first time. It was now possible to look at the landscape through large windows unblocked by doorposts.

Finally, one should mention the sleeping cars which began to run on the through night train from Euston in 1922 and continued until the closure of the Callander-Crianlarich section of the line in 1965. These were at first London and North Western vehicles of the type built during the Edwardian era, 65½ ft long, running on two six-wheeled bogies. They were for first class passengers only and had full bedding and washing facilities, and were indeed as comfortable as their present-day counterparts except for lack of soundproofing or air-conditioning. Similarly constructed LMS vehicles succeeded them, differing only in having steel panelling.

From 1929 third class sleeping cars were also run on the same train; these resembled the "couchettes" that run on Continental railways, providing four berths in each compartment which by daytime could be modified so that the upper berths were shut away against the upper wall and the lower ones provided seating. The windows on the side away from the corridor

were in groups of three, as in the usual kind of corridor carriage to which
there was an outer door, but these compartments had to be entered from the
ends of the coach; the central window let down for ventilation. A small
removable ladder beneath it permitted the users of the upper berths to
clamber up into them, though it was a bit of a stretch for the unathletic; once
there, two vertical straps kept one from falling out. There were no pre-
tensions to luxury; one was provided with a pillow and a folded blanket and
that was all. The third class supplement was only a third of what one would
have paid to sleep like a lord in the first class sleeper adjoining, whose
attendant kept an eye on the common herd in their pens and would perhaps
bring morning tea if you paid for it. Third class sleepers also ran on four-
wheel bogies, so must have been slightly noisier and rockier. As for the
morning wash, one went down the corridor for that and hoped there would
not be a queue. However, this rather Spartan accommodation met a need and
made all the difference on a long journey by night from or to the south.

　　Lastly: for a short while during the 'seventies, after the closure of the line
between Callander and Crianlarich, the Pullman Observation Car displaced
from the now-defunct "Devon Belle" was sent north, and during one
summer season ran on a daily service from Glasgow (Queen Street) to Oban
and back. An extra supplement was charged for occupying a seat in it. However, it does not seem to have proved a money-spinner, and the experiment
was not repeated.

The Pullman Observation Car, formerly used on the Devon Belle, being turned at
Oban.   *Photomatic Ltd.*

STIRLING to CALLANDER, DALMALLY and OBAN.

Fares from		Trains leave..	a.m	a.m	a.m	p.m	p.m	p.m	p.m	
EDINBURGH.	GLASGOW.	43 CARLISLE	4 18	15	9 25	..	..	7 0	..	..
1 C1 2 C1 3 C1	1 C1 2 C1 3 C1	64 EDINBURGH(WAY).	6 20	8 30	12 25	..	3 55	9 10	..	..
a. d. a. d. a. d.	a. d. a. d. a. d.	64 GLASGOW (Bu. St.)	7 15	9 15	12 35	5	..	5 30	9 20	..
..	..	..	..	64 ABERDEEN			8 55	12 30	..	4 15
..	..	..	..	67 DUNDEE (West) ..	6 55	7 40	11 10	3 30	..	4 10	6 30
..	..	..	..	67 PERTH	7 35	8 30	12 0	4	4	5 12	7 40
..	..	..	**Stirling ....leave**	8 14	10 20	2 9	5	25	9 6	32	10 32
6 6 5 0 3	3 5 6 4	6 2 8	Bridge of Allan ...	8 22	10 24	2 17	5	9 5	17 6	38 10 40
7 0 5 2 3 4	5 10 4	5 2 10	Dunblane ....arrive	8 28	10 31	2 23	5 15	22	6 43	10 46
			Dunblane ....leave	8 40	10 40	2 35	5 26	45 11 0
7 7 5 8 3 8	6 4 4	9 3 1	Doune	8 50	10 59	2 47	5 35	6 54 11 15
8 0 6 6 4	4 7 0 5	4 3 9	**Callander** arrive	9 10	11 10	3 10	5 55	7 10 11 35
			Callander.....leave	9 20	..	3 20	6 5	..	11 48
9 6 7 8 5 0	8 6	8 4 5	Strathyre	9 40	..	3 40	6 30	..	12 22
10 0 8 0 5 3	9 0 7	0 4 8	Lochearnhead	9 49	..	3 49	6 45	..	12 40
10 10 8 8 5	9 10 7	8 5 11	Killin	10 5	..	4 4	7 0	..	1 10
11 10 9 6 2	10 10 8	5 8 7	Luib............	10 21	..	4 19	7 16	..	1 32
12 10 10 9 6 8	11 9 9	0 6 0	Crianlarich	10 36	..	4 33	7 31	..	1 54
13 10 10 11 7	12 6 9	6 6 6	Tyndrum..	10 1	..	4 47	7 47	..	2 18
15 8 12 3 8	2 12 9 9	4 6 9	**Dalmally**	11 23	..	5 19	8 19	..	2 55
16 0 12 6 8	4 13 0 10 0	7	Loch-Awe	11 32	..	5 28	8 28	..	3 7
17 2 13 0 9	1 13 6 10 8	7 6	Taynuilt..........	11 53	..	5 54	8 54	..	3 42
17 9 13 6 9	4 13 9 10 9	7	Connel Ferry	12 18	..	6 10	9 11	..	4 8
18 6 14 0 9	10 14 0 11 0	8	**Oban** ..... arrive	12 40	..	6 37	9 33	..	4 35

☞ For Trossachs Coach and Loch Katrine Steamer connections see page 60.
Trains stop at Kinghouse (for Braes of Balquhidder, Loch Voyle, &c.), from Oban, on notice being given.

The passenger timetable for December 1880

OBAN, DALMALLY, and CALLANDER to STIRLING.

Trains leave		a.m	a.m	n'n	n'n	p.m	
Oban........at	..	6 0	..	12 0	5	..	
Connel Ferry	..	6 21	..	12 19	4 25	..	
Taynuilt	..	6 40	..	12 38	4 43	..	
Loch-Awe..........	..	7 6	..	1 4	5 8	..	
Dalmally	..	7 14	..	1 12	5 18	..	
Tyndrum	..	7 43	..	1 45	5 50	..	
Crianlarich	..	7 59	..	1 59	6 4	..	
Luib	..	8 4	..	2 14	6 18	..	
Killin	..	8 30	..	2 29	6 32	..	
Lochearnhead	..	8 45	..	2 44	6 46	..	
Strathyre..........	..	8 54	..	2 54	6 55	..	
Callander .... arrive	..	9 15	..	3 17	7 16	..	
Callander leave	.. 7 55	9 30	12 0	..	3 50	7 20	..
Doune........	..	8 13	9 42	12 20	4 10	7 38	..
Dunblane ..arrive	..	8 22	9 58	12 30	4 20	7 46	..
Dunblane....leave	..	8 25	10 0	12 32	4 22	7 48	..
Bridge of Allan	..	8 29	10 8	12 42	4 32	7 55	..
Stirling ..arrive	..	8 35	10 15	12 50	4 40	8 3	..
64 PERTH ....arrive	..	9 10	11 15	3 35	6 40	9 20	..
67 DUNDEE (West) "	..	9 45	12 0	4 45	7 30	10 30	..
66 ABERDEEN .. "	..	12 40	2 15	9 0	10 12	3 20	..
67 GLASGOW (Bu.St.)	..	9 30	11 24	2 10	5 50	9 20	..
67 EDINBURGH(WAY)	..	9 50	12 5	2 23	6 30	9 55	..
47 CARLISLE ..arr	..	5 7 5	7	..	8 40	12 10	..

For Loch Katrine Steamer and Trossachs Coach connections see page 60.

OBAN.

KING'S ARMS

HOTEL.

A. M'TAVISH.

VISIT

Gondie, Christie & Co.'s

FOR

Fishing Requisites,

TRAVELLING OUTFITS,

GOLF BALLS,

101 PRINCES STREET,

EDINBURGH.

Chapter Eleven

Passenger Train Services: 1880–1965

Although the Callander and Oban line provided a rail service throughout the year for the benefit of the localities through which it passed, and in particular for the people of Oban and its neighbourhood, its profitability derived from its tourist traffic. Most of the passengers it carried patronised it during the summer season, so the summer timetable always showed more trains in either direction than did that which operated for the rest of the year. The line's passenger traffic developed and eventually came to display some of the characteristics of a main line railway, with additional trains to cope with tourist traffic, vestibuled stock, special luxury accommodation, buffet and restaurant facilities *en route* and even sleeping cars.

Through services along the whole line, actually commencing at Stirling where they connected with trains from Glasgow and Edinburgh, began in the summer of 1880. The summer pattern was then of five westbound and four eastbound trains, with one fewer in each direction during the rest of the year, when each train also had fewer vehicles. Going west during the summer, and referring to departure times from Callander, the service was as follows: a train left at about midnight and ran during the small hours; a mid-morning train; one round about noon; one mid-afternoon; one during the evening. In the other direction, referring to departures from Oban, there were: an early morning train; one at about mid-morning; one at about mid-day; one in the early evening. During the autumn, winter and spring the mid-morning trains were taken off.

In 1888 through running of trains from and to Glasgow began; soon afterwards these began to carry through portions from and to Edinburgh also. Then, as tourist traffic built up, between 1900 and 1914 extra trains were fitted in between the existing ones, in the early morning, early afternoon and mid-afternoon from Callander and the late morning, early afternoon and later evening from Oban. Except for the night train, whose timings were always leisurely since it carried parcels and newspapers and made lengthy stops, timings between Callander and Oban varied by twenty minutes or so on either side of a three hour duration in either direction.

The increasing popularity of Oban as a holiday resort manifested itself also in the introduction of a special week-end train which ran there from Glasgow during the summer, beginning in 1903 and ceasing after 1911. This was the "C &O Hotel Express" – surely the only named train in this country to have included an abbreviation in its title – which was the travel element in what we would now term a package holiday. Advertisements in newspapers informed would-be holidaymakers that they could buy coupons which entitled them to travel on this train from Glasgow to one of a number of specified hotels. Of these eight were in Oban and others at Callander, Lochearnhead, Killin, Dalmally, Loch Awe, Connel Ferry, Appin, and Ballachulish; there one would be accommodated and given meals from dinner on the Friday evening to breakfast on the Monday. The total cost (it makes one's mouth water) varied from £1 6s 5d. for a third class ticket to a "B" class hotel in Callander to £2 2s 6d. for a first class ticket to an "A" class hotel in Oban itself. The train ran out on Friday evening arriving at Oban at

7.30 pm; the return was at the same time in the morning on Monday; the time taken from Glasgow was just over 3½ hours, many stops being omitted to make this possible.

A similar indication of the growth of tourist traffic was seen in the provision of through coaches from and to Euston in London, both on day and night trains, which also began in 1905 and continued till 1914. The daytime through coaches were attached to or detached from trains for the Oban line at Buchanan Street after or before a journey along the connecting line to Central Station. The night train in either direction also carried a first-class sleeping car.

When World War I broke out it was not at first evident that it was going to last as long as it did, but by the spring of 1915 this had become plain; the lights, in Sir Edward Grey's expressive phase, were going out all over Europe, and the following summer the timetable was almost the same as during the winter. There were four down trains and three up; except with the early afternoon train, however, there was no deceleration.

In 1880 and for many years afterwards there were no Sunday train services, except for the night train on Saturday night which reached Oban at about 5 am. However, in 1910 this train ceased to run on Saturday night and was replaced with one that left Glasgow on Sunday at an early hour and arrived at Oban about mid-day. There were many in Oban who frowned on this innovation as an intrusion upon the Sabbath calm, but it continued to run to the end of the line's separate existence, bringing the Sunday newspapers for the benefit of the less pious townsfolk. However, there was no corresponding up train. This service was an all-the-year-round one.

Not until 1914 were refreshment facilities provided on any of the trains, but at the beginning of August in that year the Pullman observation car *Maid of Morven* (see Chapter Ten) began to run on one train in each direction. It served only first class passengers, who paid 2s. 6d. for using it, and these could obtain drinks and refreshments at the kitchen buffet. It remained in service until the end of the following February and was then taken out, not to be used again until after the war had ended.

A revival of traffic followed the ending of the war. In 1919 the summer season saw two of the discontinued train services restored, and in 1924 a third one returned; from then until 1939 the six-each-way pattern, plus a down night train, became the pattern once more. The *Maid of Morven* came back and remained in service until 1937, attached to a down morning train and an afternoon up train. In 1923 one of the Pullman restaurant cars that had been a speciality of the Caledonian was also put into operation on the Oban line; in 1929 a second one followed. These were available for meals not only to first class passengers but also to second class travellers. Now under London Midland and Scottish ownership, they lasted until 1934, after which they were replaced by LMS pattern kitchen-restaurant cars.

The morning Sunday train service continued during and after the war without a break, and in 1931 another Sunday train, with only a few stops (and non-stop between Callander and Oban on paper, though no doubt stops were made for taking water) ran down during the morning from Glasgow and returned in the evening. In 1933 a similar train ran out from Edinburgh,

STIRLING to CALLANDER, KILLIN and OBAN.

Fares from					Trains leave..	a.m	a.m	a.m	p.m	p.m	p.m	p.m	p.m	p.m	p.m	
Mor.	Gl'gow			54	EDINBURGH(Way).	..	6 10	8 30	..	12.25	..	4 10	..	..	9 10	..
1 Cl	3 Cl	1 Cl	3 Cl	55	GLASGOW (Bu. St.)	7 10	9 20	..	1 13.	4 5	..	4 35	5 30	9 25	..	
s. d.	s. d.	s. d.	s. d.	56	ABERDEEN	..	..	..	8 55	1230	..	..	..	1 40	..	
..	..	..	..	57	DUNDEE (West) ..	6 25	7 40	..	11 5	3 30	..	..	1 10	6 40	..	
..	..	..	..	57	PERTH	7 45	8 30	..	12 0.4	5	..	..	5 13	7 35	..	
..	..	..	..		**Stirling .....leave**	8 15	1020	1215	2 14.4	58	5 20	5 37	6 30	1043	..
6 5	3 5	6 2	8		Bridge of Allan ..	8 23	1028	1223	2 22 5	5.6	26 5	45	37	1051	..
7 0	3 4	5 10	2 10		Dunblane ....arrive	8 29	1034	1229	2 28 5	10.5	31 5	51	6 45	1057	..
..	..	..	..		Dunblane ....leave	8 32	1040	1232	2 33 5	11.5	35 6	45		1110	..
7 3	8	6 4	3		Doune	8 47	1050	1242	2 43 5	19.5	44 6	10	6 54	1123	..
9 4	4 7	0 3	9		**Callander**arrive	9 7	1110	1 03	0 5	35.6	0 6	50	7 10	1145	..
..	..	..	..		Callander.....leave	9 17	1120	..	3 10	..	4 10	..	..	1158	..
6 5	0	6 4	8		Strathyre	9 37	1140	..	3 23	..	7 6	..	..	1227	..
10 0	5 3	9 0	4 8		Lochearnhead	9 47	1150	..	3 38	..	7 10	..	..	1240	..
11 2	5	11 10	2 5		Killin Junction..arr	1011	1214	..	1 3	..	7 32	..	1 27	..	
1110	6	3	1010	5		**Killin Stn.** "	1034	1237	..	4 26	..	7 53	..	..	..
..	..	..	..		Killin Pier "	1038	1 54	..	4 30	..	..	..	..	..	
..	..	..	..		Killin Pier leave	9 47	1 50	..	3 30	..	..	..	..	..	
..	..	..	..		Killin Junction "	1012	1216	..	4 4	..	7 23	..	1 29	..	
1110	6	4	10 9	5		Luib......	1029	1224	..	4 13	..	7 41	..	1 42	..	
1210	6	8	11 1	6 0		Crianlarich ...	1034	1238	..	4 26	..	7 54	..	2 4	..	
1310	f	2	2	6 6		Tyndrum	1047	1252	..	4 40	..	8 7	..	2 2	..	
15 8	5	3	12 9	6		**Dalmally**	6 40	1113	1 24	..	5 9	..	8 34	..	3 5	..
16 0	8	4	13 0	7		Loch-Awe	6 45	1121	1 34	..	5 18	..	8 42	..	3 17	..
17 3	9	1	13 6	7		Taynuilt........	7 18	1146	2 0	..	5 43	..	9 7	..	3 52	..
..	..	..	..		Ach-na-cloich	7 21	1154	3 8	..	5 51	..	9 15	..	4 1	..
17 9	9	4	13 9	f		Connel Ferry	7 29	12 1 2	15	..	5 58	..	9 23	..	4 18	..
18 6	9	1014	0	9		**Oban** .. arrive	7 50	1220	2 34	..	6 17	..	9 43	..	4 45	..

The passenger timetable for August 1886 showing the fastest journey from Callander to Oban (9.17 am & 6.40 pm) 3 hours 3 minutes and from Oban to Callander (5.25 am) 2 hours 58 minutes. Note that the 3rd Class Single Fare from Callander to Oban was 4s. 3d. This year saw the opening of the Killin branch whose connections were included in the timetable.

OBAN, KILLIN, and CALLANDER to STIRLING.

Trains leave	a.m	a.m	a.m	a.m	p.m	p.m	p.m	p.m	p.m	
Oban........at	..	5 25	8 5	10 0	..	1240	4 15	6 30		
Connel Ferry	..	5 43	8 22	1018	..	1258	4 33	6 50		
Ach-na-cloich	..	5 50	8 29	1025	..	1 6	4 40	6 57		
Taynuilt	..	5 58	8 37	1032	..	1 14	4 48	7 5		
Loch-Awe	..	6 23	9 2	1057	..	1 39	5 16	7 30		
Dalmally	..	6 31	9 10	11 5	..	1 47	5 26	7 38		
Tyndrum	..	7 9	9 38	..	..	2 14	5 55	8 7		
Crianlarich	..	7 12	9 49	..	..	2 26	6 8	8 19		
Luib..........	..	7 26	10 3	..	..	2 42	6 20	8 33		
Killin Junct.arrive	..	7 34	1012	..	..	2 51	6 29	8 42		
Killin Stn "	..	7 54	1034	..	..	3 14	6 48	..		
Killin Pier "	..	9 5	1038	..	..	3 18	..	..		
Killin Pier leave	..	..	9 46	..	..	2 55	6 30	6 56		
Killin Stn. "	..	7 17	9 50	..	..	2 26	6 8	7 12		
Killin Junction "	..	7 35	1015	..	..	2 52	6 30	8 43		
Lochearnhead	..	7 56	1035	..	..	3 17	6 51	9 8		
Strathyre	..	8 5	1044	..	..	3 27	7 0	9 18		
Callander ....arrive	..	8 23	11 4	..	..	3 43	7 20	9 36		
Callanderleave	7 50	8 30	1112	..	2 5	3 55	7 30	9 45		
Doune	8 5	8 45	1129	..	2 23	4 13	7 49	10 3		
Dunblane .....arrive	8 13	8 53	1137	..	2 31	4 21	7 57	1011		
Dunblane....leave	8 15	8 55	1139	..	2 33	4 23	7 59	1013		
Bridge of Allan ..	8 23	9 3	1147	..	2 41	4 31	8 6	1021		
Stirling ..arrive	8 29	9 10	1154	..	2 49	4 37	8 12	1028		
54 PERTH ....arrive	9 15	1110	3 20	..	..	6 40	9 20	1148		
55 DUNDEE (West) "	10 0	12 5	4 45	..	..	7 30	1030	1240		
56 ABERDEEN "	12 0	2 15	8 30	..	..	..	..	..		
57 GLASGOW (Bu. St.)	9 30	1012	1 0	..	4 35	5 43	9 18	1130		
57 EDINBURGH(Way)	9 45	1058	1 50	..	5 0	6 30	9 55	..		

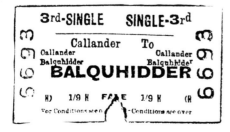

following a few minutes behind the Glasgow train. Each had a refreshment service. These ceased after 1939 and were not brought back when the war ended.

The outbreak of World War II saw a reduction in the number of trains to the same frequency of three each way as had been the case in 1914–1918, with all restaurant facilities cancelled. In 1946 only one cancelled service was re-introduced, and from then on the frequency was the same during summer and winter – five down and four up with one down morning train on Sunday. The mid-day up train and the evening down train carried restaurant cars; none of the others had any service of refreshments. One facility, however, was restored to what it had been before. The night first class sleeping car from and to Euston had returned in 1923, daily during the summer and at weekends during the rest of the year. During 1939–1945 it ran only at weekends throughout the year; in 1946–1947 it made an extra trip in mid-week; in 1949 it ran nightly during the summer and continued to do so until the Callander–Crianlarich section closed in 1965. Furthermore, in 1929 third class sleeping accommodation was also included and this facility too remained until 1965, latterly as a single composite car with full bedding facilities in the first class section and couchette accommodation in the third.

The diminution of the train service after 1946 and the gradual falling-off of custom was due of course to changing travel habits. During the period 1919–1939 the motor car, while established as a means of long distance travel, was still an expensive luxury except for the well-to-do. After World War II its use began to spread to all classes. Traffic on the Oban line never warranted more than the four daily trains provided each way after 1946, and patronage of the passenger trains by the start of the 1960s had fallen to such an extent that the closure of the line between Dunblane and Crianlarich began to be considered. Nature took a hand and blocked the line with fallen rocks in September 1965, which were not worth removing.

Little need be said about the smaller of the two branch lines, from Killin Junction to Loch Tay Pier. Passenger traffic consisted almost entirely of one or at most two coaches hauled up and down it to connect with trains on the Oban main line at the upper end or the steamer on the Loch at the lower end. In later years the line also served the needs of children from the village, when the small train made a special journey to Callander and back in the afternoon to fetch the secondary school pupils back from the High School to their homes, along with others who were put down at Strathyre and Balquhidder Junction. A journey on this train could be a lively affair at times, though the more studious preferred to sit in the same compartment and get on with their homework. Most of the trains ran through to Loch Tay station, where the locomotive ran round the coaches before drawing them back. The journey down to Killin itself took only a quarter of an hour, and the same time was taken returning; onwards to Loch Tay took another five minutes; however, there were often long waits at Killin station itself in either direction. From 1886 to 1939 the boat plied on Loch Tay, but this service did not survive World War II, and when peace returned the now disused extension to the Pier was dismantled and the line became a footpath.

One curious and short-lived experiment in the life of the Killin branch was the provision, during the summer of 1923, of a through coach from Glasgow to Loch Tay on the 9.45 am from Buchanan Street to Oban. It was detached at Killin Junction, joined on to the branch train and taken down to Loch Tay, arriving there at 1.15 pm; the return was at 6.35 pm, reaching Glasgow at 9.56 pm. This gave Glaswegians a chance to enjoy a journey by water to the lower end of Loch Tay and back. However, it does not seem to have been well-patronized, since the experiment was not repeated the next year or subsequently.

Services on the branch from Connel Ferry to Ballachulish began in the winter of 1903 as soon as the line had opened. In that year there were four northbound services and three southbound; from 1905 to 1914 there were five each way in the summer and three each way during the rest of the year. The service dropped to three trains each way throughout the year during World War I, and remained at that level until 1927, when an extra train was put on during summer Saturday evenings; this became a daily train in 1933. The onset of World War II again brought the number down to three each way throughout the year; in 1948 it rose once more to four a day with an extra one on summer Saturdays, and this remained the pattern until the line closed. There were never any trains on Sundays.

The line was worked by Drummond or MacIntosh 0–4–4 tanks hauling a few coaches which in 1912 consisted of old bogie carriages, some of which had coupé ends, but which later gave place to LMSR non-corridor coaches cascaded from lines in the south, to judge by the sepia illustrations on the compartment walls. Each train took about twenty minutes to cover the distance between Oban and Connel Ferry, where the engine ran round the train and drew it out, after it had made its connection with a train from Callander, northwards across Connel Bridge on the seventy minute journey to Ballachulish. The timings on the timetable show that the two early morning trains crossed each other at the passing loop at Benderloch, and the two mid-day trains at Creagan.

At the far end of the line there was a quay which adjoined Ballachulish station. Here for many years a steamer left three times daily to make a link with the small town of Kinlochleven, which was then very remote, with no access from the south except by this boat and rail link. During World War I German prisoners were employed to build a road from Glencoe village to Kinlochleven, and once this was completed and buses began to ply upon it the steamer service began to lose custom. Its last year of operation was 1922; after that year connections with it are no longer mentioned in the railway timetables.

No. 17396 standing at Oban Station in October 1933 on pilot duty and about to take out the coaching stock after the arrival of the express. Note the observation Pullman coach. *E.R. Morten*

Interior of observation Pullman coach *Maid of Morven* in the 'Twenties. The view from this rear panoramic window was quite spectacular and the lady is enjoying the comfort of the luxurious armchairs in July 1931. *H.C. Casserley*

STIRLING, CALLANDER, THE TROSSACHS, LOCH LOMOND, and OBAN.—Caledonian.

				Down.	Week Days.										Suns.
Miles from Stirling		Euston Station,		aft aft aft mrn	mrn	mrn aft	aft mrn		aft aft						mrn
	858	London ....dep	8 0 0 8 50 1135	.....	....12 0 5 0	....10 0		2 02 0						1135 n
	859	Edinburgh ‖ ...... "	4 06 55 9 30 1125	....1 36	....4 25	....	9 45 9 45							6 25
	858	Glasgow * .... "	4§20 7 15 10 0 12 0	....2 0 4 0 4 45	....6 10	10 0 1045								7§0
		Stirling ....dep	5 30 8 6 1050 1253	....2 52 4 48	....5 27 6 56	1150 12 0								8 30
3		Bridge of Allan .... "	5 36 8 12 1056 1 0	....2 58 4 54	....5 33 7 2	1157 12 6								8 36
5		Dunblane .... arr	5 41 8 16 11 0 1 5	....3 15 4 5 3 25 4 57 7	12 31210									8 40
	864	Perth (General)....dep	.... 7 20 9 10 1226 k	1 50 4 4 4 4 5 45	10 5 10 5									10§5
		Dunblane ....dep	5 42 8 17 11 1 1 10	....3 35 5 5 46	7 25 12 41211									8 41
8½		Doune	5 51 8 29 11 9 1 23	....3 12 5 14 5 54	7 32 1218 1223									8 51
16½		Callander .... arr	6 38 46 1124 1 41	....3 26 5 30 6 7	7 48 1235 1235									9 5
		Callander (Coach)....dep	.... 9 10 1130 i												
26½		Trossachs (Coach) ..arr	i 1040 i 10												
		Trossachs Pier†(Coach) "	i 1110 1115												
		" (Steamer)..dep													
34		Stronachlachr †(Stmr.)arr													
		" (Coach)..dep													
39		Inveranaid (Coach)..arr													
	•	" (Steamer) dep													
59½	¶	Balloch Pier(Steamer)arr													
		Callander ....dep	6 8 8 55	1 54	6 15		1245	9 10							
24½		Strathyre	6 26 9 3	2 12	6 31		1 7	9 27							
27		Kingshouse Platform :	n	n											
28		Balquhidder 893	6 31 9 21	2 18	6 38		1 12	9 33							
35½		Killin Junction ¶ 874	arr. 6 529 43 dep. 6 53 9 45	2 42 2 44	7 0 7 0		1 42 1 47								
39		Luib	7 09 52	2 53	7 9		1 55	10 2							
45½		Crianlarich 821	arr. 7 1210 3 dep. 7 1310 5	3 6 3 8	7 19 7 20		1 213 2 11		1013 1015						
50½		Tyndrum	7 231016	3 20	7 30			1025							
62½		Dalmally	7 501043	3 50	7 55										
65		Loch Awe ¶ 998	7 591049	3 58	8 1		3 10								
74		Taynuilt	8 1911 7	4 19	8 22		3 33								
77½		Ach-na-Cloich	1115	4 27											
80½		Connel Ferry 874	8 341124	4 35	8 38			1133							
87		Oban .... arr	8 55 1145	5 5	9 0		4 15	1155							

n Stop to set down on informing the Station Master at Strathyre: no Luggage or Bicycles will be taken in or put out.	k Commences on the 16th instant. § Central Station.
	n Saturday night time. ‖ Princes Street.
	a Except Sunday night.
a Stops when required to set down from Coatbridge and South thereof.	• Buchanan Street. ¶ For **Loch Awe, Loch**
	† Loch Katrine. **Lomond,** and **Loch Tay**
i Not after the 14th instant.	‡ Station for Braes of Balquhidder, **Steamers**, see page 194.
	Loch Voyle, Rob Roy's Grave, &c.

☞ For **LOCAL TRAINS** between Stirling and Dunblane, see page 859.

• For **OTHER TRAINS** between Crianlarich and Tyndrum, see page 821; between Connel Ferry and Oban, see page 874.

KILLIN JUNCTION and LOCH TAY.—Caledonian.

Mls	Down.	Week Days only.			NOTES.
		mrn mrn aft aft			
	Killin Junction ....dep	8 49 482 507 12	...		§ Killin Pier, for **Loch**
4	Killin	8 1810 33 47 26	...		**Tay Steamers,**
5	Loch Tay § .... arr	10 6 3 8	...		see page 998.

Mls	Up.	mrn mrn aft aft		
—	Loch Tay § ....dep	9 15 2 15		
1	Killin	7 359 20 2 236 40		
5	Killin Junction 870, 871 ..arr	7 489 342 376 53		

Bradshaw's timetable for 'down' trains, for October 1911, including the Loch Tay Branch.

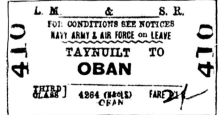

OBAN, LOCH LOMOND, THE TROSSACHS, CALLANDER, and STIRLING.—Caledonian.

Miles	Up.	Week Days only. mrn	mrn	Luncheon and Dining Car Corridor Express. (1st and 3rd class), Stirling to London (Euston). mrn	Saturdays only. aft	aft	aft	aft
	Oban ....dep.	....	6 0	9 20	....	1235	....	5 0
6½	Connel Ferry	....	6 15	9 34	....	1251	....	5 15
9¾	Ach-na-Cloich	....	....	9 43	....	1 3	....	5 28
13	Taynuilt	....	6 30	9 51	....	1 13	....	5 33
22	Loch Awe ¶ 998	....	6 49	1010	....	1 35	....	5 57
24½	Dalmally	....	6 55	1015	....	1 42	....	6 3
36½	Tyndrum	....	7 20	1042	....	2 12	....	6 31
41¾	Crianlarich 821 .... arr.	....	7 32	1052	....	2 22	....	6 41
	dep.	....	7 34	1053	....	2 23	....	6 42
48	Luib	....	7 45	....	....	2 36	....	6 54
51¾	Killin Junction ¶ 874 arr.	....	7 52	11 9	....	2 43	....	7 2
	dep.	....	7 53	1110	....	2 45	....	7 4
59	Balquhidder 894	....	8 11	1128		3 3	....	7 26
60	Kingshouse Platform ‡	....	b	....		....	....	....
62¾	Strathyre	....	8 22	1136		3 14	....	7 36
70¾	Callander ....arr.	....	8 40	1153		3 32	....	7 55
—	¶ Balloch Pier (Steamr) dep.	....	....	....		....	....	....
—	¶ Inversnaid (Steamer) arr.	....	....	....		....	....	....
	" (Coach) dep.	....	....	....		....	....	....
—	Stronachlacher † " arr.	....	....	....		....	....	....
	" (Steamer) dep.	....	....	....		....	....	....
—	Trossachs Pier " arr.	....	....	....		....	....	....
	" (Coach) dep.	....	....	....		....	....	....
—	Trossachs Hotel " "	....	....	1015 i		2 i 0	2 i 30	....
—	Callander (Coach) ... arr.	....	....	1150 i		3 i 35	4 i 5	....
—	Callander ....dep.	7 55	8 50	12 5	2 0	3 40	4 15	8 5
78¼	Doune	8 9	9 5	1219	2 14	3 55	4 29	8 20
82	Dunblane 859 ....arr.	8 16	9 14	1227	2 21	4 5	4 36	8 27
110	859 PERTH (General) ....arr.	9 10	1055	3 0	3 24	5 40	6 40	12 8
—	Dunblane ....dep.	8 17	9 15	1228	2 22	4 6	4 37	8 28
84	Bridge of Allan	8 21	9 20	1234	2 26	4 12	4 42	8 33
87	Stirling 816, 817, 864 arr.	8 28	9 28	1242	2 33	4 20	4 49	8 40
117	865 GLASGOW * ....arr.	9 17	1015	2 10	3 47	5 15	7 25	9 40
123¾	864 EDINBURGH ‖ ...... "	9c45	1030	2 17	4 35	5 40	8 10	9 52
502¾	865 London (Euston) ... "	....	7 10	1045	....	3 50	3 50	7 50

b Stops to take up on informing the Station Master at Balquhidder; no Luggage or Bicycles will be put out or taken in.
c Waverley Station, via Larbert.
i Not after the 14th instant.
* Buchanan Street.
† Loch Katrine.
‡ Station for Braes of Balquhidder, Loch Voyle, Rob Roy's Grave, &c.
‖ Princes Street.

¶ For **Loch Awe, Loch Lomond,** and **Loch Tay Steamers,** see page 998

☞ For **LOCAL TRAINS** between Dunblane and Stirling, see page 859.

*** For **OTHER TRAINS** between Oban and Connel Ferry, see page 874; between Tyndrum and Crianlarich, see page 821.

Bradshaw's timetable for the 'up' service, October 1911.

OBAN, BALLACHULISH (GLENCOE), and KINLOCHLEVEN.—Caledonian.

Miles		Week Days only. mrn	mrn	Mons., Weds., and Fris. aft	Tues., Thurs., and Sats. aft
	Oban ....dep.	8 15	11 0	5 0	8 30
6¼	Connel Ferry	8 45	1130	5 20	8 53
6¾	North Connel	8 48	1133	5 23	a
9	Benderloch	8 57	1141	5 30	9 2
16¼	Creagan	9 11	1155	5 43	9 14
19½	Appin	9 22	12 8	5 54	9 25
25	Duror	9 36	1221	6 7	9 37
28¾	Kentallen	9 44	1230	6 15	9 43
31¼	Ballachulish Ferry	9 52	1238	6 22	9 52
33¼	Ballachulish * .. arr.	9 58	1245	6 30	10 0
—	" (Steamer) dep.	10 5	1 0	....	....
—	Kinlochleven ... arr.	1125	1 40	....	....

Miles	By Steamer,	Week Days only. mrn	mrn	aft
	Kinlochleven ...dep	7 0	8 50	2 30
	Ballachulish * .. arr.	7 45	9 30	3 10
	dep.	8 0	1120	3 30
2	Ballachulish Ferry	8 5	1125	3 35
5	Kentallen	8 10	1130	3 40
8¾	Duror	8 21	1140	3 51
14¼	Appin	8 32	1152	4 4
17⅛	Creagan	8 37	12 0	4 10
24¼	Benderloch	8 56	1221	4 28
27	North Connel	9 3	1228	4 34
27½	Connel Ferry 871	9 5	1232	4 37
33¼	Oban ....arr.	9 40	1 10	5 5

a Stops to set down on giving notice to the Sta. Master at Connel Ferry. * Ballachulish (Glencoe): Sta. for Kinlochleven.

*** For **Motor Car Service** between Connel Ferry and Benderloch, see page 890.

☞ For **OTHER TRAINS** between Oban and Connel Ferry, see page 870.

The 1911, Bradshaw's service on the Ballachulish branch.

Glasgow (Buchanan Street) and Edinburgh (Princes Street) to Callander and Oban.

Down service — morning / early afternoon departures

	a.m.	a.m.	a.m.	a.m.	a.m.	a.m.	p.m.	p.m.	p.m.	p.m.
Glasgow (Buchanan Street) depart	..	4c15	6 45	..	9 45	11 30	12 10	1 5	1 40	..
Edinburgh (Princes Street) depart	..	..	..	6 45	9 25	11 30a	11 30a	12 50	1e10	..
Larbert .... depart	...	5 4	7 33	8 34	10 8	12 15p	12 46p	1 40	2 18	...
Stirling	...	6 0	7 58	8 52	10 31	12 32	1 5	2 2	2 40	...
Bridge of Allan .... „	...	5 45	8 3	8 58	10 37	12 38	1 11	2 8	2 47	...
Dunblane .... „	...	6 8	8 10	9 3	10 48	12 43	1 16	2 14	2 53	...
Doune .... „	...	6 15	8 18	9 10	10 56	12 51	1 25	2 21	3 4	...
Callander .... { arrive	...	6 29	8 33	9 25	11 11	1 6	1 40	2 37	3 20	...
Callander .... { depart	...	6 33	..	9 35	11 24	..	1 53	..	..	...
Strathyre .... „	...	6 51	..	9 53	11 42	..	2 10	..	..	...
Balquhidder .... „	...	6 58	..	10 4	11 53	..	2 20	..	..	...
Killin Junction .... { arrive	...	7 26	..	10 27	12 17p	..	2 44	..	..	...
Killin Junction .... { depart	...	7 33	..	10 29	12 20	..	2 46	..	..	...
Luib .... „	...	7 43	..	10 36	12 29	..	2 53	..	..	...
Crianlarich .... { arrive	...	7 54	..	10 46	12 40	..	3 3	..	..	...
Crianlarich .... { depart	...	7 57	..	10 48	12 42	..	3 5	..	..	...
Tyndrum .... „	...	8 10	..	11 2	1 5	..	3 17	..	..	...
Dalmally .... „	7 55	8 34	..	11 24	1 29	..	3 39	..	..	...
Loch Awe .... „	8 0	8 43	..	11 37	1 37	..	3 47	..	..	4 30
Taynuilt .... „	8 19	9 3	..	11 52	1 57	..	4 7	..	..	4 54
Ach-na-cloich .... „	8 27	..	..	12 1p	..	..	4 16	..	..	D
Connel Ferry .... „	8 35	9 18	..	12 10	2 12	..	4 25	..	..	5 11
Oban .... arrive	8 57	9 50	..	12 33	2 36	..	4 49	..	..	5 42

Notes on this half: 4c15 = Sleeping Saloon—London (Euston). The 9 45 a.m. Glasgow train conveys a First Class Pullman Observation Car, Glasgow to Oban (See Note on page 109). Through Carriage Glasgow to Loch Tay on the earlier services. "Sats. only." applies to the 12 50 / 1 5 p.m. column.

Down service — afternoon / night departures

	p.m.	p.m.	p.m.	p.m.	p.m. (Ex. Sats.)	p.m. (Sats. only)	p.m.	p.m.
Glasgow (Buchanan Street) depart	4 0	..	5 10	6 5	..	8 0	10 0	10 0
Edinburgh (Princes Street) depart	4 25	4 25	4 25	5u32	B	8 0	9 45	9 45
Larbert .... depart	4 40	5 9	5 45	6 40	..	8 45	11 33	11 33
Stirling	4 59	5 26	6 0	7 1	..	9 5	12 15a	12 15a
Bridge of Allan .... „	5 5	5 31	6 5	7 7	..	9 11	11 11p	11 11p
Dunblane .... „	5 11	5 46	6 11	7 20	7 30	9 25	12 41	12 41
Doune .... „	5 19	5 52	6 19	7 28	7 31	9 31	12 58	1 4
Callander .... { arrive	5 36	6 8	6 36	7 44	7 50	9 46	1 6	1 7
Callander .... { depart	..	..	6 45	..	..	..	1 27	1 31
Strathyre .... „	..	..	7 3	..	..	..	..	1 43
Balquhidder .... „	..	..	7 12	..	..	..	..	2 15
Killin Junction .... { arrive	..	..	7 36	..	..	..	2 7	2 15
Killin Junction .... { depart	..	..	7 38	..	..	..	2 11	2 17
Luib .... „	..	..	7 45	..	..	..	..	2 26
Crianlarich .... { arrive	..	..	7 55	..	..	..	2 34	2 43
Crianlarich .... { depart	..	..	8 2	..	..	..	2 36	2 45
Tyndrum .... „	..	..	8 12	..	..	..	..	3 6
Dalmally .... „	..	..	8 34	..	..	..	3 20	3 37
Loch Awe .... „	..	..	8 42	..	..	..	3 34	3 51
Taynuilt .... „	..	..	9 2	..	..	..	3 58	4 16
Ach-na-cloich .... „	..	..	..	..	..	..	..	..
Connel Ferry .... „	..	..	9 17	..	..	..	..	..
Oban .... arrive	..	..	9 40	..	..	..	4 50	5 4

Notes on this half: the 5 10 p.m. Glasgow train conveys a Pullman Buffet Car—Third Class—Glasgow to Oban (See Note on page 109). The 10 0 p.m. columns are "Daily except Saturdays from Glasgow" and "Saturdays only from Glasgow" respectively.

B—Will only be run when there are Passengers for Doune or Callander from Stations South of Carlisle travelling by 10.0 a.m. Train from Euston.

D—Calls at Ach-na-cloich, only when required, to set down Passengers off Loch Awe Steamer on notice being given to the Station Master at Loch Awe.

P—Trains marked P attach Vehicles *en route*, when required, and may run a few minutes later.

c—Central Station, Glasgow.   e—Leaves at 1.15 p.m. on Saturdays.   w—Waverley Station, Edinburgh.

BRAES OF BALQUHIDDER.—By previous arrangement with the Station Master at Strathyre, Passengers for the Braes of Balquhidder will be set down at Kingshouse Platform by the 9.35 and 11.24 a.m., and 1.53 and 6.45 p.m. Trains from Callander.

Falls of Cruachan.—The 4.30 p.m. Train, Loch Awe to Oban, will call at Falls of Cruachan.

No Luggage or Bicycles will be taken into or put out of the Trains at Kingshouse or Falls of Cruachan.

For Loch Tay Steamer Service and Aberfeldy Motor Service see page 139.

Killin Branch.

Down

	a.m.	a.m.		a.m.			p.m.	p.m.
Glasgow (Buchanan Street) .... depart	4c15	8 0	..	9 45	..	12 10	..	5 10
Edinburgh (Princes Street) .... „	..	6 45	..	9 25	..	..	..	4 25
Oban .... „	5 40	..	9 10	..	11 50	3 35	..	5 15
Killin Junction .... depart	7 40	10 35	11 20	12 30p	2 5p	2 55p	5 42	7 45
Killin .... { arrive	7 54	10 48	11 33	12 44	2 18	3 8	5 55	7 59
Killin .... { depart	8 45	..	11 34	1 10	..	..	6 0	..
Loch Tay .... arrive	8 49	..	11 37	1 14	..	..	6 5	..

Up

	a.m.	a.m.	a.m.	a.m.	p.m.	p.m.	p.m.	p.m.	p.m.
Loch Tay .... depart	..	10 0	..	11 50	1 30	..	..	..	6 35
Killin .... { arrive	..	10 4	..	11 54	1 33	..	..	..	6 38
Killin .... { depart	7 15	10 6	10 55	11 56	1 37	2 25	..	5 15	7 0
Killin Junction ... arrive	7 28	10 20	11 8	12 10p	1 50	2 38	..	5 28	7 13
Oban .... arrive	9 50	12 33p	..	..	2 36	..	4 49	..	9 40
Edinburgh (Princes Street) „	10 14	..	2 22p	..	..	4 44	..	8 20	9 56
Glasgow (Buchanan Street) „	9 55	..	..	1 35	..	4 30	..	8 15	9 56

c—Central Station, Glasgow.

For Loch Tay Steamer Service and Aberfeldy Motor Service see page 139.

LMS timetable for July 1923 showing the 'down' service.

Callander and Oban to Edinburgh (Princes Street) and Glasgow (Buchanan Street).

							Sats. only.					Sats. only.							
		a.m.	a.m.	a.m.	p.m.	a.m.	a.m.	p.m.	p.m.		p.m.	p.m.				p.m.		
Oban ....dep.		5 40	9 10	10 0		11 15	11 50	P			3 35	5 15				6 25		
Connel Ferry .... „		5 56	9 26	10 16		11 32	12 10p				3 52	5 23				6 41		
Ach-na-Cloich .... „			9 34	10 24			12 18					5 41						
Taynuilt.......... „		6 10	9 43	10 33		11 49	12 27				4 6	5 50				6 56		
Loch Awe .... „		6 30	10 3	10 55		12 11p	12 47				4 28	6 10				7 16		
Dalmally .... „		6 37	10 10			12 19	12 55				4 36	6 18				7 24		
Tyndrum .... „		7 5	10 41			1 26					5 5	6 49				7B52		
Orianlarich ..... { arr. dep.		7 14 7 15	10 54 10 56			1 35 1 37					5 15 5 17	6 58 7 0				8 3 8B4		
Luib .... „		7 26	11 7			1 48						7 6				8B13		
Killin Junction . { arr. dep.		7 33 7 35	11 16 11 18			1 57 1 59					5 35 5 37	7 19 7 23				8B22		
Balquhidder .... „		7 52	11 38			2 16			3 50		5 54	7 45				9 41		
Strathyre .... „		8 2	11 44			2 27			3 57		6 3	7 55				8B48		
Callander ..... { arr. dep.	7 55	8 20 8 31	12 0 12 8p		1 52 2 2	2 44 2 53		4 5	4 13 4 40		6 20 6 32	8 10 8 22				9 5 9 10		
Doune .... „	8 9	8 45	12 8p	1 55		3 7		4 19	4 54		6 48	8 34				9 24		
Dunblane .... „	8 16	8 52	12 29	2 2	2 20	3 14		4 26	5 1		6 55	8 41				9 31		
Bridge of Allan .... „	8 22	8 58	12 35	2 7		3 20		4 35	5 6		7 1	8 46				9 36		
Stirling .... „	8 28	9 4	12 42	2 13	2 30	3 26		4 41	5 12		7 8	8 52				9 42		
Larbert .... „	8 42	9 19	12 57	2 38	2 49	3 47		5b46	5 46		7 28	9 16				11d23		
Edinburgh (Prin. St.) arr.	9w48	10 14	2 22			4 44	6 40	6 40			8 20	10 5						
Glasgow (Buch. St.).. „	9 18	9 55	1 35		3e25	3 25	4 30	6 22	6 22		8 15	9 56				12c17d		

B—Calls only when required to pick up Passengers for Stirling and beyond.
P—Trains marked **P** attach Vehicles *en route*, when required, and may run a few minutes later
b—Arrives at 5.7 p.m. on Saturdays.   *c*—Central Station, Glasgow.
d—Arrives at 10.52 p.m. on Saturdays.   *e*—Arrives at 3.53 p.m. commencing 8th September.
†—Daily except Saturdays.   *w*—Waverley Station, Edinburgh.

FALLS OF CRUACHAN.—The 10.0 a.m. and 3.35 p.m. Trains from Oban will call at Falls of Cruachan.

BRAES OF BALQUHIDDER.—The 5.40 a.m. and 5.15 p.m. Trains from Oban and 3.50 p.m. Saturdays only Train from Balquhidder will call at Kingshouse Platform to take up Passengers from the Braes of Balquhidder when there are any such on the Platform, but the Train will not call to set down Passengers. Passengers must be on the Platform at the time the Train is due to leave Balquhidder Station.

No Luggage or Bicycles will be taken into or put out of the Train at Falls of Cruachan or Kingshouse.

For Loch Tay Steamer Service and Aberfeldy Motor Service see page 139.

Pullman Observation Car.—The Observation Car on the 9.45 a.m. Train from Glasgow (Buchanan Street) to Oban and the 3.35 p.m. Train from Oban to Glasgow (Buchanan Street) is available for First Class Passengers only on payment of a Supplementary Fare as under ;—

Between **Glasgow** and Intermediate Stations to Doune inclusive, and **Oban** and Intermediate Stations West of **Callander**, ...   **2s. 6d.**
Between **Glasgow** and Intermediate Stations to **Callander** inclusive, ...   **1s. 6d.**
Between **Callander** and Intermediate Stations to **Oban** inclusive, ...   **1s. 6d.**

Passengers holding Third Class Tickets may have Meals supplied in the Third Class Compartments of the Carriage adjoining the Observation Car.

Pullman Third Class Buffet Car on 9.10 a.m. Train from Oban (commencing 3rd September) and 11.15 a.m. Train from Oban (until 1st September inclusive), also 5.10 p.m., Glasgow to Oban, is available for Passengers holding Third Class Tickets on payment of Supplementary Fares as under :—

Between **Glasgow** and Intermediate Stations to Doune inclusive, and **Oban** and Intermediate Stations West of **Callander**, ...   **2s. 0d.**
Between **Glasgow** and Intermediate Stations to **Callander** inclusive, ...   **1s. 3d.**
Between **Callander** and Intermediate Stations to **Oban** inclusive, ...   **1s. 6d.**

Passengers holding First Class Tickets may have Meals supplied in the First Class Compartments of the Carriage adjoining the Pullman Buffet Car.

Ballachulish Branch.

		a.m.	Ex. Sats. B a.m.	Sats. only. p.m.	
Glasgow (Buch. Street). . . depart			8 0	12 10	5 10
Edinburgh (Princes Street) .... „			6 45	11 30a	4 25
Oban .... „		8 5	11 50	5 15p	9 0
Connel Ferry ....depart		8 38	12 20p	5 42	9 23
North Connel.......... „		8 41	12 23	5 45	A
Benderloch.......... „		8 46	12 28	5 50	9 36
Creagan .... „		9 7	12 44	6 6	9 55
Appin .... „		9 17	12 53	6 15	10 4
Duror .... „		9 30	1 4	6 26	10 16
Kentallen .... „		9 38	1 12	6 33	10 23
Ballachulish Ferry .... „		9 47	1 19	6 40	10 31
Ballachulish (Glencoe) for Kinlochleven ....arrive		9 55	1 27	6 48	10 40

		a.m.	a.m.	p.m.	
Ballachulish (Glencoe) for Kinlochleven .... depart		7 15	10 25	4 15	
Ballachulish Ferry .... „		7 20	10 30	4 20	
Kentallen .... „		7 25	10 35	4 25	
Duror .... „		7 37	10 45	4 35	
Appin .... „		7 48	10 56	4 46	
Creagan .... „		7 55	11 3	4 53	
Benderloch .... „		8 11	11 19	5 9	
North Connel .... „		8 19	11 27	5 17	
Connel Ferry .... „		8 30	11 30	5 23	
Oban .... arrive		8 57	12 33p	5 58	
Edinburgh (Princes Street) .. „		2 22p	4 44	10 5	
Glasgow (Buch. Street). „		1 35	3e25	5 5c	

North Connel Station.—This station will be used as a " Halt," and the Trains will only call there for the purpose of setting down and picking up Passengers.

The Attendant at the Bridge will issue Third Class Single Journey Tickets to Connel Ferry Station and Third Class Single and Return Journey Tickets to Oban to Passengers joining South-going Trains, and Third Class Single Journey Tickets to Benderloch station to Passengers joining North-going Trains, and Passengers travelling beyond these points will re-book to their destination.

Heavy Luggage, Perambulators, Bicycles, etc., or Parcels Traffic will not be conveyed to or from North Connel Station, and Passengers making use of the Platforms will require to take charge of any Light Luggage which may be accompanying them.

BARCALDINE SIDING.—All Trains between Connel Ferry and Ballachulish (Glencoe) call at Barcaldine Siding, when required, to pick up or set down Passengers.

A—Calls at North Connel, when required, to set down Passengers on notice being given to the Station Master at Connel Ferry.

B—Will run specially on Saturday, 14th July.

e—Commencing 3rd Sept., arrives Glasgow (Buchanan Street) at 4.30 p.m.

For Motor Service between Ballachulish (Glencoe) and Kinlochleven see page 140.

LMS timetable for July 1923 showing the 'up' service.

GLASGOW (BUCHANAN STREET) AND EDINBURGH (PRINCES STREET) TO CALLANDER, FORT-WILLIAM AND OBAN.

WEEK DAYS.

London (Euston)............dep.		k7|30	7 20	...	10|50				11 5	12|15		1| 5	1|40	...	1|47	...
Glasgow (Buch. Street)... ,,		4c|15	7 20	...	8 0	10 0	...			11 58			1|23	...	1|10	...
Edinburgh (Princes St.).. ,,		.	7 0	...	7 0	9 25	...										
Larbert ....dep.		8 1	7 53	...	8 53	10 6	...	12|10	12|50	...	1|38	2|14	...	2|28	...
Stirling .... ,,		8 45	8 10	...	8 48	10 51	...	12|27	1 6	...	1|52	2|37	...	2|46	...
Bridge of Allan............... ,,			8 16	...	8 53	10 56	...	12|32	1|11	...	1|57	2|42	...	2|52	...
Dunblane .... ,,			8 23	...	9 1	11 4	...	12|38	1|18	...	2| 3	2|50	...	2|59	...
Doune....................... arr.			8 31	...	9 10	11 11	...	12|46	1|26	...	2|10	3| 0	...	3| 7	...
Callander................{ dep.		8 12	8 44	...	9 23	11 26	...	12|59	1|40	...	2|26	3|21	...	3|24	...
Strathyre .... ,,		8 28	...	...	9 30	...	...		1	48	...			...		...
Balquhidder................... ,,		8 35	...	...	9 48	...	...		2	5	...			...		...
Killin Junction............{ arr. dep.		8 57 6 58	...	...	9 58 10 20 10 21	...	...		2	19 2	42 2	43	...			...		...
Luib .... ,,		7 4	...	...	10 26	...	...		2	49	...			...		...
Crianlarich .... arr.		7 15	...	...	10 38	...	...		3	0	...			...		...
Crianlarich ....dep.		7 41	...	...		...	...		3	59	...	Stop		...		...
Spean Bridge....... arr.		9 34	...	...		...	...		7	54	...			...		...
Fort-Augustus(B)... ,,		10 40	...	...		...	...		s08	55	...			...		...
Fort-William ......,,		9 51	...	...		...	...		8	11	...			...		...
Crianlarich ....dep.		7 16	...	...	10 39	...	...		3	13	...			...		...
Tyndrum....................... ,,		7 28	...	...	10 55	...	...		3	35	...			...		...
Dalmally....................... ,,		7 50	...	...	11 20	...	...	1	25	3	43	...			...		...
Loch Awe..................... ,,		7 58	...	...	11 28	...	...	1	30	4	1	...			...		...
Taynuilt...................... ,,		8 16	...	...	11 44	...	...	1	50	4	10	...			...		...
Ach-na-Cloich............... ,,		8 24	...	...	11 54	...	...	1|58	4|17	5|13	5|18		...		...
Connel Ferry................. ,,		8 35	...	...	12| 3	...	...	2| 5	4|36	5|33	5|35		...		...
Oban....................... arr.		8 54	...	...	12	26	...	...	2	24					...		...

WEEK DAYS—continued.   SUNDAYS.

London (Euston)............dep.		4| 5		5|12	5|30	10 0	8| 0	8| 0	10| 0	2| 0	80|10|50		7e|15
Glasgow (Buchanan St.) ,,		3w|25	5| 3			6| 8	7|50		10|20	10|45	10|20	...	10c|15
Edinburgh (Princes St.).. ,,						5w|39				10|20	7 10		
Larbert ....dep.		4|39		5|46	6|11	6|42	8|43	8|43	11| 2	11|18	8 17	...	10 57
Stirling .... ,,		4|57	5|52	6| 0	6|28	7| 2	9| 3	9| 3	11|17	11|48	8 50	...	11 14
Bridge of Allan............... ,,		5| 2		6| 5	6|33	7| 7	9| 8	9| 8	11|22	11|22	8 55		
Dunblane .... ,,		5| 8	6| 1	6|13	6|42	7|13	9|20	9|25	11|31	12| 2	9 1		
Doune....................... arr.		5|15	6|10	6|19	6|49	7|20	9|28	9|31	11|37	12|12	9 9		
Callander................{ dep.		5|29	6|26	6|36		7|34	9|43	9|43	11|54	12 29	9 27	...	11 45
Strathyre .... ,,		...		6	42		...	...			12 32	9 30	...	11 50
Balquhidder................... ,,		...		6	58		...	...			12 53	9 48		
Killin Junction............{ arr. dep.		...		7|10 7|34 7|35		...	...			1 33 1 35	9 58 10 23 10 24		
Luib .... ,,		...		7	41		...	...				10 31		
Crianlarich .... arr.		...		7	52		...	...			2 0	10 43		
Crianlarich ....dep.		...		7	53		...	...						
Spean Bridge....... arr.		...		8	4		...	...						
Fort-Augustus(B)... ,,		...		8	27		...	...						
Fort-William ......,,		...		7	10		...	...			2 1	10 44		
Crianlarich ....dep.		...		7	53		...	...			3 0	10 58		
Tyndrum....................... ,,		...		8	4		...	...			3 15	11 29		
Dalmally....................... ,,		...		8|27		...	...			3 45	11 33	1|48	
Loch Awe..................... ,,		...		8	35		...	...				11 52		
Taynuilt...................... ,,		...		8|53		...	...			4 7	12|18		
Ach-na-Cloich............... ,,		...		9| 7		...	...			4 31	12|30	2|20	
Connel Ferry................. ,,		...		9	27		...	...						
Oban....................... arr.		...		9	27		...	...						

B—Motor Bus Service from Spean Bridge.
S O—Saturdays only.
b—Calls, when required, to set down Passengers from South of Carlisle on notice being given at Stirling.
c—Central Station, Glasgow.
k—Saturday nights excepted.

f—Commencing November 2nd, departs Crianlarich 7.46 a.m., arrives Spean Bridge 9.37 a.m. and Fort William 9.54 a.m.
w—Waverley Station, Edinburgh.
For particulars of Trains calling at Falls of Cruachan and Kingshouse see page 529.

KILLIN BRANCH.

WEEK DAYS.

									8X				
Glasgow (Buchanan St.)..dep.	...	4c|15	...	8 0	...	...	12|15	...	11 58		5|12	...	...
Edinburgh (Princes St.).. ,,	...		...	7 0	...	...	11 58	...			5| 3	...	...
Oban........................... ,,	...	6 5	...	...	9 10	12 5	...	4|55	...	s05|15	...	...	...
Killin Junction............dep.		8 5		10 25		11 13		2 6	2|47	6|58		7|40	
Killin ....{ arr. dep.		8 19		10 38		11 26		2|19	3 0	7|11		7|54	
Loch Tay.................. arr.													

WEEK DAYS.

								8X	80	8X			
Loch Tay.................dep.	...	...											
Killin ....{ arr. dep.	...	7 45	10 0	10 55		1|42	2|25	7| 0	7|17				
Killin Junction............ ,,	...	7 58	10 14	11 8		1|56	2|38	6|52 7| 1	7|13 7|30				
Oban........................... arr.	...		12|26				4|36		9|27	9|27			
Edinburgh (Princes St.).. ,,	...	10 55		1|45		4|38		9|43	9|49				
Glasgow (Buchanan St.).. ,,	...	10 5		1|34		4|27		9| 9	9|41	10b|45			

b—No connection after October 9th.
SO—Saturdays only.
c—Central Station, Glasgow.
SX—Saturdays excepted.

LMS timetable for September 1936 showing the 'down' service.

OBAN, FORT-WILLIAM AND CALLANDER TO EDINBURGH (PRINCES STREET) AND GLASGOW (BUCHANAN STREET).

WEEK DAYS.

Oban ....dep.	...	6 5	...	8 10	9 10	...	...		12 5					4 55	5 15
Connel Ferry ...... ,,		6 20		8 20	9 26				12 24						5 31
Ach-na-Cloich......... ,,					9 35				12 33					5 20	5 42
Taynuilt .... ,,		6 34			9 42				12 39					5 29	5 49
Loch Awe............. ,,		6 53		10 1					12 58					5 49	6 9
Dalmally .... ,,		7 0			10 8				1 5					5 56	6 16
Tyndrum............... ,,		7 27			10 36				1 32					6 24	6 45
Crianlarich .... arr.		7 40			10 50				1 42					6 34	6 55
Fort-William ..dep.									9 54					4 10	4 10
Fort Augustus (C) ,,									8 27					3 17	3 17
Spean Bridge...... ,,									10 12					4 23	4 23
Crianlarich ...... arr.									12 9					6 17	6 17
Crianlarich ....dep.		7 41		10 21					1 43					6 35	6 56
Luib .... ,,		7 50		11 0					1 52					6 44	7 6
Killin Junction....... ,,		8 0		11 10					2 3					6 54	7 15
Balquhidder............ { arr.		8 1		11 11					2 3					6 55	7 17
{ dep.		8 17		11 27					2 20					7 15	7 42
Strathyre .... ,,		8 26		11 35					2 30					7 23	7 50
Callander............... { arr.		8 43		11 53					2 47					7 40	8 8
{ dep.	7 55	8 46	9 47	12 2		1 25	1 40		2 55	4 0	4 5	5 43		7 46	8 24
Doune................... ,,	8 7	8 58	9 24	12 15		1 42	1 52		3 7	4 12	4 17	5 55	7 0	7 56	8 24
Dunblane .... arr.	8 16	9 8	9 33	12 24		1 50	1 59		3 16	4 21	4 26	6 4	7 8	8 7	8 32
Bridge of Allan .... ,,	8 22	9 26		12 31		1 55	2 4		3 21	4 26	4 38	6 9	7 14	8 11	8 38
Stirling .... ,,	8 28	9 17	9 41	12 37		2 1	2 10		3 27	4 37	6 15		7 20	8 17	8 44
Larbert .... ,,	8 42	9 33	10 1	12 55		2 27	2 42		3 46	4 53	4 53	6 36		8 36	9 3
Edinburgh (Prin. St.) arr.	9w45	10 55	10 55	1 45					4 38			7 27		8 25	
Glasgow (Buch. St.) ... ,,	9 14	10 5	10 42		1 34	3 14	3 14		4 27	5 58	5 58	7 9		8 19	9 9
London (Euston)....... ,,		7 0	7 0		10 40				D5 0	4 50	5 0			6u55	9 41

WEEK DAYS.

SUNDAYS.

Oban ....dep.		6 35		8 55	9 35				6 0
Connel Ferry .... ,,		6 53		9 10	9 51				
Ach-na-Cloich............. ,,		7 8		10 7					6 30
Taynuilt .... ,,		7 16		10 7					
Loch Awe................. ,,		7 34		10 23					
Dalmally .... ,,		8 0		10 35					
Tyndrum..................... arr.		8 17							
Crianlarich ....dep.									
Fort-William ....dep.									
Fort Augustus (C) ,,									
Spean Bridge...... ,,		8 18							
Crianlarich ....dep.		8 25							
Luib .... ,,		8B35							
Killin Junction........... ,,		8 52							
Balquhidder................. ,,		9B 0							
Callander................... { arr.		9 15							8 32
{ dep.		9 16				10 12			8 34
Doune....................... ,,		9 28				10 24			
Dunblane .... ,,		9 37				10 33			
Bridge of Allan .... ,,									
Stirling .... ,,		9 45				10 41			8 59
Larbert .... ,,		10 12				11 14			9 15
Edinburgh (Prin. St.) arr.		10 45				12z13			
Glasgow (Buch. St.) ... ,,		7 45				8 0			c10 3
London (Euston)....... ,,									

B—Calls, when required, to pick up Passengers for Stirling or South thereof on notice being given.

C—Motor Bus Service to Spean Bridge.

D—Arrives at 4.50 a.m. on Sundays.

E—Calls at Ach-na-cloich, when required, to pick up Passengers for Stirling or South thereof on notice at Ach-na-cloich not later than 6.30 p.m.

b—Commencing November 2nd leaves Fort William 10.3 a.m., up at Bridge 10.51 and arrives Crianlarich 12.11 p.m.

e—Central Station, Glasgow.

s—Arrives at 7.45 a.m. until October 11th.

w—Waverley Station, Edinburgh.

Brae of Balquhidder.—By previous arrangement with the Station Master at Strathyre, Passengers for the Brae of Balquhidder are booked to Kingshouse Platform by the 9.30 a.m., 1.48 p.m. and 6.42 p.m. Trains from Callander.

Brae of Balquhidder.—The 6.5 a.m., 4.55 and 5.15 p.m. Trains from Oban will call at Kingshouse Platform to take up Passengers from the Brae of Balquhidder when there are any such on the Platform, but the Trains will not call to set down Passengers. Passengers must be on the Platform at the time the Train is due to leave Balquhidder Station.

No Luggage or Bicycles will be taken into or put out of the Trains at Kingshouse.

Falls of Cruachan.—The 9.35 p.m. (Saturdays only) Train from Oban, and 12.15 p.m. (Saturdays only) Train from Dalmally will call at Falls of Cruachan.

BALLACHULISH BRANCH.

WEEK DAYS

Glasgow (Buch. St.)...dep.	4c15	...	8 0	...	12 15	5 12			
Edinburgh (Princes St.) ,,		...	7 0	...	11 58	5 6			
Oban .... ,,	8 10	...	12 5	...	4 55	8 55			
Connel Ferry ....dep.	8 45		12 27		5 20	9 20			
North Connel .... ,,	8 45		12 30		5 23	A			
Benderloch .... ,,	8 53		12 51		5 44	9 45			
Creagan..................... ,,	9 9		12 51		5 44	9 51			
Appin....................... ,,	9 16		12 58		5 51	9 66			
Duror....................... ,,	9 27		1 17		6 10	10 9			
Kentallen .... ,,	9 35		1 17		6 16	10 19			
Ballachulish Ferry......... ,,	9 41		1 24		6 16	10 27			
Ballachulish (Glencoe)									
for Kinlochleven ...... arr.	9 47		1 29		6 22	10 33			

Ballachulish (Glencoe)									
for Kinlochleven ......dep.	7 30	11 0			4 0				
Ballachulish Ferry...... ,,	7 34	11 4			4 4				
Kentallen .... ,,	7 40	11 10			4 10				
Duror .... ,,	7 50	11 30			4 30				
Appin....................... ,,	8 1	11 31			4 31				
Creagan..................... ,,	8 8	11 38			4 38				
Benderloch .... ,,	8 22	11 52			4 52				
North Connel .... ,,	8 28	11 59			4 59				
Connel Ferry .... arr.	8 31	12z1	2		5 2				
Oban .... arr.	8 54	12 26			b5 35				
Edinburgh (Princes St.) ,,	1 45	4 38			d9 43				
Glasgow (Buch. St.) ... ,,	1 34	4 27			e9 9				

Barcaldine Siding.—All Trains between Connel Ferry and Ballachulish (Glencoe) call at Barcaldine Siding, when required, to pick up or set down Passengers.

A—Calls at North Connel when required, to set down Passengers on notice being given at Connel Ferry.

b—5.33 p.m. on Saturdays.

c—Glasgow (Central) Station.

d—9.49 p.m. on Saturdays.

e—9.41 p.m. on Saturdays.

LMS timetable for September 1936 showing the 'up' service.

Glasgow, Edinburgh and Callander and Oban

		F			N		Sats only								N					Ex Sats	Sats only			SUNS
Glasgow . lev.	a.m.	a.m	a.m	a.m	a.m	a.m	p.m	p.m	p.m	p.m	p.m	p.m	p.m	p.m	p.m	p.m	p.m			p.m			a.m
Buchanan St.	4c20	7 15	8 0	9 45	1010	11 0	1212	1 *5	—	2 25	4 0	5 10	6 10	8 0	10 0	1015				10 0			7c15
Edinburgh (P.St.)	.	6 54	6 54	9 20	9 20	.	a1144	1 10	.	1 10	.	4 23	5V23	.	9 45	1124				9 45			.
Stirling _ _ _	5 45	8 12	8 50	1032	11 3	1228	1 7	2 15	.	3 21	4 58	6 17	10 9	3	1059	1124				12E1a			8 35
Dunblane . .	—	8 25	9 3	.	1116	1240	1 20	2 23	.	3 34	5 10	6 14	7 23	9 25	1112	1140				1213			8 47
Doune . .	—	8 31	9 10	.	1122	1246	1 29	2 34	.	3 40	5 16	6 20	7 29	9 31	1118	1146				1222H			8 54
Callander arr.	6 10	8 44	9 23	1039	1135	1 0	1 41	2 47	.	3 53	5 28	6 32	7 42	9 44	1132	12 1				1244H			9 11
Callander lev.	6 12	—	9 33	11 5		Stop	1 49	—	.	4 5	—	6 37	—	—	—	—				1248			9 15
Strathyre	—	—	9 51				2 7	—	.	4 23	Stop	6 55	—	—	—	—				1 9			9 33
Kingshouse Plat.	—	—	9A57				2A12	—	.	4A29	—	7A0	—	—	—	—				—			.
Balquhidder .	6 36	—	10 0	1130			2 16	—	.	4 33	—	7 5	—	—	—	—				9 43			
Killin Junct. arr.	6 58	—	1023	1155			2 41	—	.	4 56	—	7 27	—	—	—	—				.			.
Killin Junct. lev.	6 59	—	1025	1157			2 42	—	.	4 57	—	7 29	—	—	—	—				.			.
Luib _ _ _	7 5	—	1031				2 48	—	.	5 3	—	7 35	—	—	—	—				1016			
Crianlarich lev.	7 16	—	1042	1213			2 59	—	.	5 14	—	7 45	—	—	—	—				2 25			1028
Tyndrum _ _	7 28	—	1054	1225			3 12	—	.	5 28	—	7 58	—	—	—	—				—			1043
Dalmally . .	7 54	—	1117	1247			3 34	—	.	5 54	—	8 21	—	—	—	—				3 19			11 7
Loch Awe .	7 59	—	1125	1257			3 42	—	.	6 3	—	8 29	—	—	—	—				3 38			1117
Taynuilt .	8 17	.	1143	1 17			4 0	—	.	6 20	—	8 47	—	—	—	—				4 6			1137
Ach-na-Cloich .	8 26	—	1153	.			4 9	—	.	6 27	—	8 56	—	—	—	—				.			.
Connel Ferry .	8 38	.	12 3	1 34	3 57	.	4 21	—	.	5 13	6 48	3*10	9 4	—	—	—				4 42			1155
Oban _ _ arr.	8 55	—	1227	1 51	4 21	.	4 38	—	.	5 36	7	5	8*27	9 21	—	—				5 5			1215

					Sats only								Sats only	SUNS
	a.m	a.m	a.m	a.m	a.m	p.m	a.m	p.m	p.m	p.m	p.m	p.m	p.m p.m	
Oban _ _ _ _ lev.	—	6 58	10	.	9 10	.	9 50	12 5	—	4 0	4 50	5 15	6 30	9 0	.
Connel Ferry . .	—	6 21	8 26	.	9 28	.	10 9	1225	—	4 20	5 6	5 34	6 50	9 21	.
Ach-na-Cloich . .	—	—	—	.	9 36	.	1017	1233	—	4 28	—	5 42	—	—	.
Taynuilt _ _ _	—	6 34	—	.	9 42	.	1024	1239	.	4 34	—	5 49	7 3	—	.
Loch Awe _ _	—	6 53	—	.	10 1	.	1048	1258	.	4 53	—	6 8	7 22	—	.
Dalmally _ _	—	7 0	—	.	10 8	.	.	1 5	.	5 0	—	6 15	7 29	—	.
Tyndrum _ _	—	7 30	—	.	1036	.	.	1 33	.	5 28	—	6 43	7 57	—	.
Crianlarich lev.	—	7 42	—	.	1051	.	.	1 43	.	5 41	—	6 53	8 11	—	.
Luib _ _	—	7 52	—	.	11 2	.	.	1 53	.	5 51	—	6 53	—	—	.
Killin Junction arr.	—	8 2	—	.	1112	.	.	2 3	.	6 1	—	7 13	—	—	.
Killin Junction lev.	—	8 4	—	.	1114	.	.	2 4	.	6 2	—	7 14	—	—	.
Balquhidder . .	—	8 20	—	.	1130	.	.	2 20	.	6 18	—	7 34	8 44	—	.
Kingshouse Platform	—	8B25	—	.	.	.	.	2B27	.	6B24	—	—	—	—	.
Strathyre . .	—	8 29	—	.	1140	.	.	2 31	.	6 28	—	7 43	—	—	.
Callander . . arr.	—	8 46	—	.	1158	.	.	2 48	.	6 55	—	8 0	9 9	—	.
Callander . . lev.	7 55	8 53	—	9 25	12 8	1 25	.	2 55	5 43	7 0	—	8 5	9 10	—	.
Doune _ _ _	8 7	9 5	✓	9 37	1220	1 44	.	3 7	4 12	5 55	7 12	—	8 15	9 30	.
Dunblane _ arr.	8 16	9 14	.	9 46	1229	1 54	.	3 16	4 21	6 4	7 21	—	8 24	9 38	.
Stirling _ _ n	8 28	9 25	.	9 54	1240	2 7	.	3 27	4 33	6 16	7 33	—	8 35	—	.
Edinburgh (Pr.St.) n	9V50	11 5	.	11 5	3 2	.	.	4 46	6V41	7 40	9 V 3	—	10 4	—	.
Glasgow (Bu. St.) n	9 15	1015	n	1	1 34	3 8	.	4 23	5 27	7 13	8 25	—	9 31	1030	.

* Saturdays only   † Except Saturdays   c Central Station
A Stops to set down on notice at Strathyre. Luggage and Bicycles not dealt with
B Stops to take up when Passengers on Platform. Luggage and Bicycles not dealt with
E Will not be detained beyond 12·15 a.m. for connection with 1·0 p.m from London (Euston)
F Sleeping Car from London (leave 7·30 p.m) to Oban on Tuesday and Friday nights only
H Stops on notice at Stirling to set down from Carlisle and South thereof, or on notice to take
     up for Strathyre and beyond   K Stops to set down passengers on notice at Stirling
N Through Carriage Edinburgh to Oban
SC Sleeping Car   **TC** Through Carriage   V Waverley Station

---

Connel Ferry and Ballachulish.

Mls		a.m	a.m	a.m	p.m	p.m			a.m	a.m	E	p.m	p.m
.	Glasgow (Buchanan St.)lev.	4c20	E 8 0	1212	5 10		Ballachulish N _ _ lev.	7 30	1050	2p45	4 0	7 0
.	Edinburgh (Princes St.) n		6 54	1144a	4 23		Ballachulish Ferry . .	7 34	1054	2 49	4 4	7 4
.	Oban _ _ _ _ n	8 10	9 50	12 54	50	9 0	Kentallen _ _ _	7 40	11 0	2 55	4 10	7 10
.	Connel Ferry . . lev.	8 45	1010	1227	5 15	9 30	Duror	7 50	1110	3 6	4 20	7 21
.	North Connel _ _ _	8 48	1013	1230	5 18	9 33	Appin	8 1	1121	3 16	4 31	7 31
2½	Benderloch b _ _ _	8 53	1018	1235	5 23	9 38	Creagan b _ _	8 8	1128	3 23	4 38	7 38
10	Creagan b _ _ _ _	9 9	1033	1261	5 39	9 54	Benderloch b _ _ _	8 22	1142	3 47	4 52	7 52
13½	Appin _ _ _ _ _	9 16	1040	1258	5 46	10 1	North Connel _ _ _	8 28	1149	4 4	4 59	7 59
18	Duror _ _ _ _ _	9 27	1051	1 9	5 57	1012	Connel Ferry _ arr.	8 31	1152	3 47	5 2	8 2
22½	Kentallen _ _ _ _	9 35	1059	1 17	6 5	1020	Oban . . . arr.	8 55	1227	4 21	5 36	8 27
25½	Ballachulish Ferry _ _	9 41	11 7	1 23	6 11	1026	Edinburgh (Princes St.) n	3 2	4 46	9VB3	10 4	—
27½	Ballachulish N _ _ arr.	9 47	1113	1 29	6 17	1032	Glasgow (Buchanan St.) n	1 34	4 23	8B25	9 31	—

* Saturdays only   † Except Saturdays   c Central Station
‡ Except Mondays   § Mondays only   E Ceases after 28th September
A Wednesdays only   F Saturdays 5-35 p.m.
B From 9th September arrive Edinburgh (Princes   K 2 minutes later on Tuesdays and Saturdays
    St.) 10-4 p.m.; Glasgow (Buchanan St.) 9-31 p.m.   N Ballachulish is the station for Glencoe and
b Barcaldine Siding (situate between Benderloch   Kinlochleven
    & Creagan)—All Trains stop on notice to take   T Tuesdays only   X 2 mins. later on Saturdays
    up or set down   V Waverley Station

L.M.S. timetable for October 1946.

Table 33

GLASGOW (Buchanan Street), EDINBURGH (Princes Street), STIRLING, KILLIN, BALLACHULISH and OBAN

Week Days

Miles from Glasgow		
32	Glasgow (Buchanan St.) dep	
32	Edinburgh (Princes St.)	
32	Stirling	
35¼	Dunblane	
39	Doune	
46¼	Callander	
55	Strathyre	
57	Kingshouse Platform	
58	Balquhidder	
65¼	Killin Junction (Exchange Platform only)	
69¼	Killin	
69¼	Luib	
75½	Crianlarich (Lower)	
80¼	Tyndrum (Lower)	
87	Dalmally	
95¼	Loch Awe	
104½	Taynuilt	
107¾	Ach-na-Cloich	
111	Connel Ferry	
111¼	North Connel	
114	Benderloch	
116	Creagan	
121	Appin	
124¼	Duror	
133¼	Kentallen	
138¾	Ballachulish Ferry	
138¾	Ballachulish	
117¾	Oban	

British Railways timetable for September 1961 showing the 'down' service.

Notes:

- **A** Except Mondays
- **a** Stops to take up when passengers are on platform. Heavy luggage and bicycles not dealt with
- **B** not dealt with
- **C** Stops to set down on notice at Strathyre; luggage and bicycles not dealt with
- **D** Diesel Service
- **E** or E Except Saturdays
- **G** Dep 4 23 pm on Saturdays
- **J** Stops to set down from stations East of Dalmally on notice at that point. Heavy luggage and bicycles not dealt with
- **K** From Glasgow (Central) Station
- **L** Calls on notice to take up or set down

- **S** Saturdays only
- **SC** Sleeping Car
- **TC** Through Carriage
- **T** Stops to set down on notice to guard
- **X** Saturdays only and depart Edinburgh (Waverley). Via Dunfermline
- **Z** Ballachulish is the Station for Glencoe and Kinlochleven
- **2** Second class only

- **#** From Glasgow (Buchanan St.) on Sunday nights until 10th December, 1961 inclusive and from 20th May, 1962. From Glasgow (Queen St.) on Sunday nights from 17th December, 1961, until 13th May, 1962 inclusive

- **p** pm
- **Q** Calls at Barcaldine Halt
- **RB** Buffet Car
- **RC** Restaurant Car

For OTHER TRAINS between Crianlarich and Tyndrum, see Table 34

Table 33—
continued

OBAN, BALLACHULISH, KILLIN, STIRLING, EDINBURGH (Princes Street) and GLASGOW (Buchanan Street)

Week Days only

Arr Ballachulish
10 59 pm

Arr Oban
8 30 pm

Arr Ballachulish
6 31 pm

SC Oban to London (Euston (arr 7Ǝ37 am) daily until 23rd September inclusive;
Mondays only commencing 25th September
TC Oban to Glasgow and Edinburgh
RB Observation Car Oban to Glasgow until 23rd September, 1961 inclusive

Arr Oban
5 35 pm

TC Oban to Glasgow and Edinburgh   **RC** Oban to Glasgow

TC Callander to Glasgow

TC Oban to Glasgow

TC Callander to Edinburgh

Arr Ballachulish
10 7 am

Arr Oban
8 48 am

TC Oban to Glasgow and Edinburgh

TC Callander to Glasgow

Miles from Ballachulish / Miles from Oban

Oban	dep
Ballachulish Z	dep
Ballachulish Ferry	
Kentallen	
Duror	
Appin	
Creagan	
Benderloch	
North Connel	
Connel Ferry	arr / dep
Achn-a-Cloich	
Taynuilt	
Loch Awe	
Dalmally	
Tyndrum (Lower)	
Crianlarich (Lower)	
Luib	
Killin	dep
Killin Junction (Exchange Platform only)	arr / dep
Balquhidder	
Kingshouse Platform	
Strathyre	
Callander	arr / dep
Doune	
Dunblane	
Stirling	arr
Edinburgh (Princes St.)	arr
Glasgow (Buchanan St.)	

Miles from Killin / Miles from Oban

For OTHER TRAINS between Tyndrum and Crianlarich, see Table 34

B Stops to take up or set down on notice at
Connel Ferry. Heavy luggage and bicycles
not dealt with
b Stops to take up when passengers on
platform. Luggage and bicycles not dealt
with
C Passengers can arr Edinburgh (Waverley)
9 41 am, change at Larbert and Polmont

D Diesel Service
E Except Saturdays
K Arr 8 17 pm on Saturdays
L Calls on notice to set down or take up
N Stops to set down only on notice at Connel
Ferry
p pm

Q Calls at Barcaldine Halt
RB Buffet Car
RC Restaurant Car
S Saturdays only
SC Sleeping Car
TC Through Carriages
U Arr 7 52 am on Sunday mornings 17th and
24th September
Y Arr Edinburgh (Waverley)

X Via Dunfermline and arrives Edinburgh
(Waverley)
Z Ballachulish is the station for Glencoe and
Kinlochleven
❷ Second class only

British Railways timetable for September 1961 showing the 'up' service.

A "Jumbo" No. 57339 on the one-coach branch line train about to leave Killin for Killin Junction. The hill in the background is Meall non Tarmachan (1043 metres).

N. E. Stead Collection

Callander Station from the east on the occasion of a visit by the preserved Caledonian 4−2−2 No. 123 with a special train of two preserved coaches in Caledonian colours. One wonders how the photographer managed to position himself as there was no footbridge: did he climb a signal post?

N. E. Stead Collection

Chapter Twelve
Accidents and Mishaps

The Callander and Oban line, both as an independent company and later as a part first of the LMS grouping and then of British Railways, has luckily been free from major train accidents. No passenger has ever been killed or seriously injured anywhere on its system. Moreover, what accidents to trains *have* occurred mostly took place during the first seven years of the completed line's existence.

The first happened in the Pass of Brander on 17th August, 1881. The ten o'clock passenger train from Oban to Dalmally was passing the Falls of Cruachan, 6 miles east of Taynuilt, when it was struck by a boulder rolling down the hillside. The impact derailed a number of the short four-wheeled coaches, but no injury was suffered by anyone on the train, which was going at a slow speed as had been recommended by the Board of Trade's inspector when he had passed the line for use the previous year. He had foreseen the possibility of a rock-fall down the side of Ben Cruachan and had suggested that a 25 mph limit be observed along Loch Awe-side and through the Pass of Brander. His caution was now seen to be justified, and a little later the wire fence along the north side of the track in the most risky part of the route was constructed (see Appendix Two).

The next accident occurred on 13th April, 1883. The 6.37 am down train from Callander to Oban, a mixed train composed of locomotive and tender, eight goods wagons, a brake van (in which a guard was travelling), a single composite coach and a passenger brake coach, was approaching Strathyre when the eighth wagon left the rails and began to oscillate violently; soon after that the other vehicles to its rear also left the rails. Brakes had now been applied and the train came to a halt. No one had been hurt, but the derailed wagon and the two rear passenger vehicles were slightly damaged; considerable damage was done to the track, 450 chairs, 160 sleepers and one rail being broken, two rails being bent.

Major-General Hutchinson, the Board of Trade inspector sent to report on the incident, attributed the mishap to faulty springs on the wagon which had begun to oscillate. The guard in the brake van immediately behind had noticed its antics, but had not thought fit at once to apply his brakes, for which error of judgement he was duly reproved. The inspector singled out for special criticism the practice of running mixed trains with the wagons in front of the passenger coaches, which meant that the continuous brake in the latter section was not under the driver's control. "I submit," he concluded, "that the Directors of the Caledonian Railway should . . . consider how far they are justified in running mixed trains over a line possessing the precipitous character of the Callander and Oban Railway."

The third accident, which could have been a very bad one occurred on 26th June, 1886 somewhat to the east of Dalmally. A special excursion train from Falkirk to Oban, of twelve well-filled coaches, most of them four-wheelers and all brand-new, hauled by two locomotives and running an hour late, was recovering speed round a curve just beyond Succoth viaduct. After slowing to 15 it had reached 25 mph on a downhill gradient of 1 in 75, when the eighth vehicle left the rails; the coupling between it and

Dunalastair Class II, No. 14328 seen here at Balquhidder Station taking water in September 1933; a rare visitor to this line and *below* the locomotive now on its train of mixed stock waiting to commence its journey.   *E.R. Morten*

the coach behind them broke. The front part of the train came to a standstill 200 yds further on; the rear part left the rails, tilted to the left and scraped an embankment before coming to rest with some of its coaches leaning over at 45 degrees against the bank. Two passengers complained of slight injury but all were able later to proceed on their journey. Eight vehicles were slightly damaged; 300 chairs and 97 sleepers required replacing.

Major Marindin, the Board of Trade inspector sent to investigate the accident, found that what had happened was that a stay rod which had run longitudinally along the left hand side of the leading brake van had come adrift at one end, presumably because the nuts and bolts securing it at that end had become loosened; these latter could not be found and might have worked loose some distance back. The rod had trailed along the track bed and at one point thrown up a hard piece of stone which rested on one of the rails; the next wheel to pass this point had become derailed and set in motion the sequence that made up the accident. He noted that, while the coaches had been inspected at Callander by an examiner, there had been pressure on the latter not to delay the already-late train, so only the right hand side of the coaches had been examined. If, the inspector thought, the nuts had already worked loose on their bolts, the examiner would probably have noticed this; in his opinion the "corner-cutting" at Callander might well have been a contributory cause to the accident. He also observed that a really serious calamity had been avoided by only a matter of seconds, for if the rear coaches had tilted over that much earlier they would have fallen over the side of a bridge into a stream, and there might have been a considerable toll in deaths and injuries.

Derailments were not uncommon during these early days. As mentioned in Chapter Ten, Brittain's "Radial Tanks" were always misplacing their wheels and having to be put back on to the line during 1880–1881. On 24th August of the latter year one of Connor's 0–4–2 goods engines which replaced them was derailed with seven vehicles at the points which led to the Loch Awe pier. Six days later, at the same place, the 5.30 am from Oban had, quite exceptionally, three locomotives at its head, and the second engine ran off the rails and dragged the third one after it; it then damaged 80 yds of track before coming to rest. The driver had found he could not use his brakes; so had whistled for his fellow-enginemen to use theirs; it was later discovered that the offending engine's wheel tyres had been so badly worn on one side that those on the other side had had to bear far more than their proper share of the weight, and the load imposed was more than the light 70lb./yd rail could bear.

As to accidents to other railway structures: the first decade also saw a bridge washed away during a storm in November 1882. This was the bridge across the Nant, a burn which descended to Loch Etive just to the east of Taynuilt station. The company put up a temporary wooden structure in its place, and then followed as long as four and a half years while a new bridge was constructed. The new bridge was very substantially built, with two spans taking the place of the original single span, and wrought-iron longitudinal and cross-girders between substantial masonry abutments. The middle piers were cast-iron cylinders filled with concrete. Major Marindin from the Board of Trade passed the structure as satisfactory in the middle of April in 1887. It is still in use today, just a hundred years later.

Coming now to a much later period: the only train fire to have occurred on this line was in August 1948, while an up train was descending Glen Ogle. One of the gangway connections was found to be alight. The whole train was hastily evacuated of its passengers while the blaze was put out; they then re-embarked and proceeded.

The Callander and Oban line has not suffered from snow-storms in the way that its neighbour, the West Highland Line, has been plagued; unlike the latter it has never had to erect snow fences. During the winter of 1947, however, when fearful wintry weather afflicted the whole of the British Isles for weeks on end, the night train from Callander to Oban became stuck one night near Glenlochy crossing. It was double-headed and while the train engine lodged itself in a drift its pilot got free, snapping the coupling and going on on its own. It was a little while before the pilot engine's crew realised what had happened. Very sensibly they kept going until they reached Dalmally, where they waited. The train engine's crew eventually decided to try to break through and follow, and one hopes that such passengers as were on the train were given warning of what was to follow. The train set back for a hundred yards and then charged the snowdrift. There was a great deal of slipping and snow flew everywhere, and eventually they pushed through the drift and proceeded. The thing to watch for now was the pilot engine; it was impossible to see more than a few yards ahead, so the intrepid guard placed himself between the smokebox and the buffer beam, shone his lantern forwards and tried to see through the gloom, while the crew inched the engine cautiously along. After a while the guard's lantern went out, and he had to rely on his straining eyes. Dalmally was reached at last and feeling enormous relief the two crews greeted each other; the pilot was re-attached and the train proceeded.

Finally the two runaways must be mentioned. The first has already been alluded to in Chapter Seven. In 1947 the down morning goods train from Callander could not manage the 1 in 60 gradient through the Pass of Leny, and stuck fast near the top, over two miles from Callander. In such circumstances the guard was required to walk back down the track and place detonators on the line, to warn any train that might approach from behind. As he did so, for some reason the train parted in the middle and the rear portion ran back, gathering momentum rapidly as it descended the steep gradient. The 7.55 am passenger train was standing in the platform at Callander when the runaway trucks cannoned into it. No one was hurt, but there was a pile up beneath the over-bridge which was destroyed.

To the second runaway I can give no date; I merely recall its happening at some time shortly before the closure of the Callander to Crianlarich section; it may have been in 1963 or 1964. A goods train was proceeding during the night eastward towards Glenoglehead. Somewhere just short of the summit a number of trucks broke away from the back of the train. On the steep gradient which they had already surmounted they ran back, gathering speed. I cannot recall hearing of any death or injury in connection with this incident; the guard presumably must have jumped clear after failing to bring the broken-off tail of the train to a halt. It had some 6 miles of falling gradient to traverse, and one can only conjecture what the speed may have been when Luib, at the bottom of the gradient, was reached. There were now another 6 or so more or less level miles to Crianlarich, on which the runaway could slow down. It eventually came to rest just beyond Crianlarich Junction, a short distance from my house; we were away at the time and heard nothing, but on our return there was visible evidence that the trucks had indeed travelled that far, for there was a deep groove in every sleeper where something projecting downwards from one of the vehicles had left its mark. I have been unable to find any official reference to this occurrence, but my memory assures me that it certainly happened, and was the talk of Crianlarich village for some days afterwards.

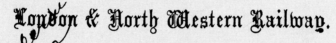

London & North Western Railway.

(Cir. K 373.)

EUSTON STATION, LONDON, N.W.,

February 9th, 1886.

The Caledonian Company's Shed and Office

at Oban were completely destroyed by fire on the

night of the 4th inst., and all the books, in

connection with the working of the traffic, burnt.

Please, therefore, send to Mr. Grant, Goods

Agent, Oban, as early as possible, copies of all

invoices you have issued or received for traffic to

and from Oban since the 1st January last.

F. HARRISON,

Chief Goods Manager.

Another sort of accident!

Crianlarich Lower Yard seen here on the 20th April, 1988 with No. 37413 marshalling the timber traffic alongside the old station platform, before propelling the completed train out to join the old North British line to Glasgow, via the connecting curve.

N.E. Stead

No. 37422 seen here west of Crianlarich, heading for Oban on the 20th April, 1988. In the background, the last snows of the winter cling to the slopes of Ben More.

N.E. Stead

Chapter Thirteen

Partial Closure and the Disused Lines To-day

The immediate closure of the section of the Callander and Oban line, together with the branch from Dunblane to Callander, was precipitated by a fall of earth and stones north of Balquhidder station, but the writing had been on the wall for some years previously. In 1951 the line between Comrie and Balquhidder was closed, which removed a feeder of traffic originating in Perth and to the east and north-east and directed towards Oban; travellers from these parts now had to take the longer and more expensive route by way of Dunblane. So some custom was lost. More deleterious was the growth of private motoring during the Macmillan "Never-had-it-so-good" years. If you already possessed a car (however much it might cost to obtain and maintain) it was cheaper to use it when two or more persons had to travel than purchasing rail tickets, and much more convenient because of all the luggage you could stow in the boot or on the back seat. While during the summer months the line was still moderately well-patronized, during the rest of the year it was a different story. The line which had survived Dr Beeching's basilisk gaze had now become a liability to British Rail; surgery was needed so that the only viable part could continue – the part west of Crianlarich junction.

This decision had already been taken in principle when in 1964 freight traffic ceased to be routed through Callander, and was sent up the West Highland line and then down the Crianlarich spur on its way to Argyll. A year later it was announced that passenger trains would take the same route and the forty miles between Dunblane and Crianlarich would be closed. Fewer people protested in Callander than might have been expected; however, they enjoyed a frequent bus service to Stirling, which mitigated the inconvenience. At Killin there was more of an outcry. The railway link by way of Killin Junction was more important to them since they had no good bus service, and while secondary school children who travelled daily to Callander High School and back during term time could no doubt be (and were) taken in a special bus, parents did not think that 44 miles' road travel each day would help their children's educational progress. Children, too, disliked the idea; you could do some at least of your homework on a train, but not on a bus. However, it was no good grumbling; British Rail could not be expected to keep maintaining and operating 22 miles of railway for the sake of a few children.

Elsewhere along the route there were no outcries. It was all very sad, no doubt, and "the end of an auld sang", but no doubt buses would ply to take the place of the vanished trains. (In fact they never did). Then, unexpectedly, Nature had the decisive word. A fall of rock occurred in Glen Ogle on Monday, 27th September, 1965, which blocked the permanent way with huge boulders five weeks before the designated closure date. Inspection showed not only that removing the tumbled rocks would be costly, but also that the hillside was in a dangerous state, and there might be further falls. So the line was closed there and then.

West of Crianlarich no one minded at all. Trains were still going to run from Glasgow to Oban, as many as before, but they would now travel directly over a route 16 miles shorter than the roundabout one by way of Dunblane, and, so it turned out, much more cheaply. From Oban to Glasgow it was now to cost 9s. less, return fare, than before. To Edinburgh it was the same amount dearer, and also now involved a change at Glasgow Queen Street and a heel-kicking wait. But no one in Glasgow worried much about that. Queen Street now became, and has remained ever since, the rail gateway to Oban. Buchanan Street, whence all the trains had started in former times, was now fated to be closed and dismantled; eventually a bus terminal arose on its site.

A year later the Ballachulish branch also came under the axe. Passenger receipts from it had begun to decline even as early as the 'thirties, when the old road from Tyndrum to Glencoe and Fort William rough, narrow and steeply-pitched in places (part of it has now been included in the West Highland walkway), was reconstructed along a different route so that heavy and fast traffic could use it. The tolls payable at Connel Ferry railway bridge could now be avoided by folks who lived in Appin and on Loch Levenside. In June 1965 all freight traffic was removed from the Ballachulish branch. As to passengers, they were few indeed if one excluded the school children going to and from Oban. In March 1966 the line closed completely. On the last day before this happened some sort of remembrance-event – one scarcely knows what to call it – took place at Oban station, when the last train left for Ballachulish. What had been intended as a solemn wake turned into a high-spirited carnival, doubtless with some alcoholic assistance, and the *Oban Times* commented that it was more like the celebration of a line's opening rather than a solemnity at its closure. Thus, after little more than 60 years, the trains ceased to run and the trackbed was left to Nature, apart from some sections which were to be buried under tarmac as part of the County's road-improvement schemes.

Some parts of the disused sections of the line are worth following on foot at the present day. However, the Ballachulish branch must really be counted out; it was built so close to the public road that there is no advantage in using the old trackbed except for one ½ mile section. Here, where the A828 road goes under the southern arch of the bridge across the narrows of Loch Creran, a walker – and cyclist, too, if his machine is not too heavily burdened with luggage – can scramble up to the old rail embankment by a well-worn track and turn left to reach the bridge itself, where a metal-floored walkway parallels where the track used to be. A quarter of a mile further on along the embankment there is another steep slope down to the road again. In this way one can save a 6 mile detour round the head of the loch. There has been talk of converting the bridge for road traffic, but it is not at all certain now that the structure would stand the strain; however it should last for a while yet before it becomes unsafe for pedestrians.

One ought also to spare a mention for the imaginative adaptation of the old Kentallen station, which is now a guesthouse and restaurant. The dining room occupies the space between the platforms and affords splendid views of Loch Linnhe and the hills of Morven on the other side. If one sleeps there for a night one may very well find oneself in a bedroom which was once the old waiting room, remodelled now so that it is only just recognizable. Photographs of railway scenes on the wall indicate the owner's sympathies.

As for the line between Callander and Crianlarich, there are two parts worth walking, one fairly short, one much longer. The 6 miles between the bridge over the river at the northern end of the Pass of Leny and the village of Strathyre for the most part follow the western shore of Loch Lubnaig. One passes the site of St Bride's Crossing, and a group of log houses built by the Forestry Commission for holiday use, and then there is solitude until the outskirts of Strathyre village are reached. The main A84 road is only ⅓ mile away, but the traffic on it is almost inaudible. Two miles from Strathyre one can diverge if one wishes to a bridlepath where the going is a little easier. Refreshments can be had in Strathyre itself.

Within the last few months a footpath has been made along the former track bed from Callander to St Bride's and this extends the walkway very scenically. Occasional 'buses ply between Callander and Strathyre, so that the 9-mile walk can be done conveniently in one direction alone.

From Strathyre to the site of the former Balquhidder Junction station the route follows the main road closely, and in places the latter's recent re-routings have obliterated it. From a point ¼ mile from Balquhidder station, however, (Grid Reference 7212 2576) one can climb on to the embankment and follow the line as it ascends at 1 in 60 right up to the summit at Glenoglehead. (For a walker, of course, such a gradient is practically the same as level ground). The trackbed has by now become a smooth path, the slag fragments from the ballast being now trodden down so that even in ordinary walking shoes the going is not tiresome. There is one obstacle to be circumvented, where a farm structure has been erected and surrounded with a fence; after that there are no difficulties. A short stone viaduct carries one across the Kendrum burn; one then goes under an ornamental metal foot-bridge built to link one part of the Edinchip estate with another. Then the track curves round the shoulder of Meall Reamhar and turns north-west to climb the western flank of Glen Ogle.

At about G.R. 7231 2583, when the path is now at a considerable altitude above Loch Earn, the prospect down its whole length begins to open up and can be enjoyed at intervals for about ¾ mile, though the trees which have grown up along the trackside obliterate the view in places. The path then parallels the Ogle burn and the A84 road from Lochearnhead to the summit; between the road and the burn General Wade's road, now grass-green, stands plainly out. Two viaducts are then crossed, one short and one much longer. The main road, climbing more steeply than the line did, is now drawing nearer on the right, and if one wishes one can join it. Otherwise one continues past the small Loch Larig Eala to the left and four railway houses to the right which mark the site of the former Killin/Glenoglehead station.

Beyond the latter the path begins to descend, passing beside young conifer plantations and swinging sharply round to the west. A mile further on one sees where the former Killin branch came in from the north-east. Killin Junc-tion is now a mere space between trees; every railway structure has van-ished. The trackway continues between conifers, leaves the woods to cross the Ardchyle burn by a stone viaduct (where the slag fragments underfoot make the traverse rather uncomfortable). It then descends along the bare

Tyndrum Station today with its small glass waiting shelter; compare with photographs on *pages 45 and 46.* *Author*

Taynuilt Station in April 1988 with No. 37413 approaching with a Glasgow freight.
N.E. Stead

The remains of Ach-na-Cloich Station as seen in 1988. *Author's Collection*

Connel Ferry Station as seen in its reduced state in 1988. Compare with *pages 54 and 94.* *Author's Collection*

hillside, giving sweeping views across Glen Dochart to the hills beyond, and crosses the Ledcharrie burn by another stone viaduct before reaching the A84 road at the site of the former Luib station, now a caravan park.

The next 6 miles to Crianlarich are scarcely worth following since they go too close to the road, and in places merge with it where it has been reconstructed. It is better to get a lift to Crianlarich, or take the late afternoon postbus, and find Youth Hostel or bed-and-breakfast accommodation there, or else to take an earlier postbus (at about 3.30 pm) to Killin, where there is also a Youth Hostel and plenty of hotel and guest-house accommodation. Callander, Strathyre, Balquhidder and Lochearnhead can also put up wayfarers, though they have no Youth Hostels. The whole walk from Balquhidder to Luib is a long day's excursion; that from the Pass of Leny to Strathyre can be done comfortably in an afternoon.

The Killin branch itself is hardly worth the effort, but if one is staying at Killin it is worth spending a fine evening walking through the village to the point where the line crossed the South Loch Tay road (G.R. 7327 2572) and then following the track across the Dochart and Lochay bridges. The walk continues past the former site of Killin station along what has become a recognised village footpath to the site of the old Loch Tay station, which with its pier has now vanished. One can return to the village along the road beside the tree-shrouded Finlarig Castle.

No. 37037 on service 1T28 (Oban to Glasgow) seen here between Tyndrum Lower Station and Crianlarich on the 17th August, 1985. The West Highland Station of Tyndrum Upper is just visible above the front of the locomotive.   *N.E. Stead*

Chapter Fourteen

The Oban Branch: 1965 to the Present Day

Since the landslide in Glen Ogle and the subsequent re-routing of the trains between Glasgow and Oban by way of Crianlarich Upper Station, what is left of the Callander and Oban Railway has become an offshoot of the former West Highland Railway, with advantages and disadvantages to the traveller. The advantage of a much quicker and shorter journey to Glasgow, with better connections to the South, no doubt outweighs the somewhat longer journeys that have to be made to Edinburgh and towns in Central Scotland. Of the former Callander and Oban Railway some 42 miles remain. One of its halts, Ach-na-Cloich, has long been closed and its wooden buildings are slowly mouldering away; another, Falls of Cruachan, was also disused for a long time but was re-opened in 1987 on an experimental basis. Loch Awe station was also closed for many years but has now re-opened as a single unstaffed platform, and it is possible once again to alight there and sail on the Loch in a motor launch which plies during the summer months. The number of daily trains in either direction first dwindled to three, but has now gone up to four since the beginning of the present year (1989). The down night train continued for a while as the 1 am from Glasgow, but ceased to run nine years ago. (I once travelled on it during the winter, was the only passenger, and was invited to sit in the locomotive's driving compartment as it was warmer there!) Altogether, a come-down from the palmy days of the years before World War I.

There have been changes in other respects. While the trains still make connections with the ferry services to Mull, those with steamer services on the larger lochs are now a thing of the past. The steamers have been scrapped long ago; the coach services which enabled the circular tours to be made have vanished into history. But the rail link is still there and despite road competition is holding its own. As always since its inception it is busy during the summer and comparatively little used during the winter. In July and August trains are always well-filled and sometimes packed. The actual journey over what is left of the line is more comfortable than ever. Only standard class travel is now available, as on all other Scottish branch lines, but it is always adequate; wide windows offer much better views than the little oblong lights of past days, and there is always a toilet compartment within reach.

Diesel locomotives were beginning to replace the "Black Fives" when the closures took place in 1965, and until the beginning of the present year were the only form of traction on regular scheduled trains. At first Class 27s were used; later Class 37s took over, dull blue with yellow noses, in some cases named after local features and all sporting the little Highland terrier badges. They ran through from Glasgow to Oban. It was usual for drivers to exchange places when trains going in opposite directions met at a passing loop; it was not customary for one man to cover the whole 100-mile journey.

The coaches used until the beginning of 1989 were usually BR Mark 1 or Mark 2a vehicles, either open or compartmented, in rakes of six during the tourist season and of three or four during the rest of the year, except at

Christmas, the New Year and Easter. During the summer a mini-buffet on each train provided basic snack food, though not over the whole route. The attendant travelled out from Glasgow to the point where the train he was on crossed with another, and then transferred his vending trolley across the platform to the train going the other way. The usual change-over point was Crianlarich Upper station, where there was also (and still is) an excellent refreshment room which unlike the train buffet, operates throughout the year. It is the only one now left on the whole line once one has left Glasgow, and snacks may be had at moderate prices in clean and cheerful surroundings while one awaits a train. It is an advantage now, since the introduction of the new Sprinter service, that the trains wait five minutes at Crianlarich; there is more time in which passengers proceeding further can make their purchases.

The pattern of trains which operated until January 1989 was as follows throughout the year. (1988 times are given).

Down:				Up:			
Glasgow (Q.St) dep:	08.34	12.04	18.34	Oban: dep.:	08.10	12.50	18.10
Crianlarich arr.:	10.29	13.57	20.30	Crianlarich arr.:	09.19	13.59	19.19
dep.:	10.32	14.03	20.33	dep.:	09.21	14.01	19.21
Oban: arr.:	11.44	15.16	21.46	Glasgow (Q St) arr.:	11.14	15.58	21.14

Stops were made at all stations between Crianlarich and Oban. The times in both directions between these two stations were faster than they had ever been — an indication of the diesels' superior powers of acceleration and ability to run fast uphill. The first and second down trains and the second and third up trains linked with the daily ferries to and from Mull, and if the latter were running late on their return there was enough leeway in the rail schedules to allow time to be made up from a late start — especially during the off-season when the locomotive might be hauling little more than its own weight.

Crianlarich Lower station was closed in 1965 and all trains were then routed by way of the spur, which now became part of the branch. About half a mile of the former line has been left in place, pointing in the Callander direction, as a single track connection leading back to several sidings on the site of the old station. To these latter logs from neighbouring forests are brought by road and loaded on to timber wagons which are taken away from time to time, being backed up the spur to the upper line and hauled off to a pulping mill. The elaborate track layout which formerly existed at the junction between Crianlarich East and West signal boxes has now vanished with the boxes themselves. All signals and signal posts have also disappeared since the new system of signalling, described in Chapter Seven came into operation. The track layout at Crianlarich Upper station has also been considerably simplified, and it is no longer possible for a train to leave that station for Oban if another is on the section between Tyndrum Lower and Crianlarich.

Every station along the line except Oban is now unstaffed and tickets have to be bought on the train. A policy is being followed of removing or closing station buildings and substituting glass shelters. This is not altogether welcomed by the local inhabitants, particularly at Taynuilt, where a campaign is being waged to save the old station buildings which date from the opening of the line. The new station at Oban, described above in Chapter Seven, has the advantage of being new and clean, but facilities are cramped and there is no longer a large covered concourse. If, as sometimes happens, a down train is very badly delayed, those who come to travel back in it to Glasgow may be forced to wait on the unsheltered platform.

Apart from those at Dalmally and Taynuilt, all passing loops have now been dismantled, but "Anderson's Piano" is still in place and operative.

The circular tours in which trains, loch-steamers and horse-drawn coaches connected with one another are now a thing of the past, but the branch's scenic properties have recently been recognized in a new way. During the summer season weekend excursions from the south, using first-class stock with restaurant cars and with meals provided at every seat, have been routed to Oban, time being allowed there for excursions before returning. These are naturally not cheap, including as they do the provision of hotel accommodation.

Even more expensive, aimed at millionaires rather than the merely "well-off", is the "Royal Scotsman", the ultimate in luxury rail travel in this country. This really is something to gape at. It is a privately-organized train which hires the locomotive that pulls it and the track it runs on. It operates during the summer and until the end of October, and each tour occupies a week, running out from and back to Edinburgh Waverley station and visiting those parts of the Scottish Highlands that are accessible by rail. Its farthest points of penetration are Oban, Mallaig and Kyle of Lochalsh. The whole train of eight vehicles consists of refurbished stock from former days, one coach being nearly 100 years old. Remodelled sleeping cars, in which each pair of first class compartments have been knocked into one, permit each user to repose at night in a small bedroom. Meals are taken in reconditioned restaurant cars adorned with spotless napery and fresh flowers in vases; one car is of London and North Western origin; the other originally ran on the Great Northern line out of Kings Cross. There are also a lounge car and an observation car. All have been painted in the former London and North Western livery except for the Great Northern vehicle which retains its varnished teak exterior.

The train traverses the Oban branch on Wednesday of each week of the season when it operates, returns the same evening, and is stabled overnight, being shunted for that purpose into the wood-sidings at Crianlarich, where a special platform has been built to allow passengers to alight and stretch their legs in the village the following morning. The price per person for the full week's tour, with excellent cuisine and enthusiastic young uniformed attendants, who travel in their own special coach, is not far short of £2000. One recalls that the "Northern Belle", which ran from and to London during the 'thirties of this century, offering a similar week's experience, cost £20, though it has to be admitted that one then slept in ordinary first class sleeping compartments, not in double-sized ones. It seems a pity that the "Royal Scotsman" cannot be steam-hauled, as the "Northern Belle" was.

Two freight trains run down the branch and back again each weekday; they are hauled by Class 37s and are never heavy. They always include some oil-tank wagons bound to or from the Connel oil terminal.

The "Sprinter Revolution" reached the Oban branch, as also the Fort William and Mallaig branches, on January 23rd, 1989, and the service pattern changed completely. Instead of six locomotive-hauled trains leaving Glasgow daily, three for Oban and three for Fort William, one being the through sleeping-car service from London, with a corresponding six trains in the other direction, the provision now is four daily departures from Queen Street, each train comprising two two-coach Super-Sprinter units, one for Oban and one for Fort William. At Crianlarich the units separate. The front one proceeds to Oban, the rear one waits for a few minutes longer and then goes on up the West Highland line to Fort William where it either reverses and continues to Mallaig, or connects with another Sprinter for the same destination. Thus, despite there being two fewer daily departures from Glasgow, there is actually one extra service along either branch from Crianlarich onwards. The return daily pattern is the mirror image of the outward one, the units recoupling at Crianlarich. The sleeping car service precedes all the Sprinter trains going northwards, and omits to call at Glasgow, so from Helensburgh onwards arrivals are an hour earlier than before, though the London departure time is unchanged. Returning, the sleeper is two hours later all the way from Fort William to Helensburgh; again it misses out Glasgow and reaches London at the same time as before. The new timetable is as follows (intermediate station times being omitted):

Down: Weekdays:							*Sundays:*		
Euston	d.	21.00[1]							21.00
Glasgow (Q.S.)d.			8.10	12.10	16.40	20.22	16.40	20.22	
Helensburgh	d.	5.44	8.47	12.46	17.16	21.04	17.16	21.04	5.44[2]
Crianlarich	a.	6.55	9.50	13.51	18.20	22.15	18.20	22.15	6.55[2]
	d.		9.55	13.56	18.25	22.20	18.25	22.20	
Oban	a.		11.04	15.04	19.33	23.26	19.33	23.26	
Crianlarich	d.	6.57	9.59	14.00	18.29	22.24	18.29	22.24	6.57[2]
Fort William	a.	8.55	11.43	15.43	20.15	00.06	20.15	00.06	8.55[2]

1. Except Saturday nights. 2. Monday Morning arrivals.

Up: Weekdays:							*Sundays:*		
Fort William	d.	6.47	12.04	15.57	19.47	20.20[3]	15.57	19.47	20.20
Crianlarich	a.	8.35	13.48	17.41	21.36	22.18[3]	17.41	21.36	22.18
Oban	d.	7.30	12.35	16.28	20.25		16.28	20.25	
Crianlarich	a.	8.41	13.43	17.36	21.31		17.36	21.31	
	d.	8.46	13.56	17.46	21.41	22.22[3]	17.46	21.41	22.22
Helensburgh	d.	9.50	14.57	18.50	22.42	23.27[3]	18.50	22.42	23.27
Glasgow (Q.S.)a.		10.27	15.43	19.27	23.25		19.27	23.25	
Euston	a.					8.14[4]			8.14[4]

3. Except Saturday nights. 4. Arrival following morning.

In the case of every train except the 12.35 up from Oban times are faster than they have ever been, despite the Sprinter units each having less than half the horse-power of a Class 37 diesel locomotive. The reason for this paradox is that a Class 37 engine had to haul its own weight as well as that of its train.

I made an experimental journey from Crianlarich to Oban and back on the first day of the new service. Each coach has some sixty seats. Not all face across tables; about half of them are arranged aircraft-seat fashion, but the latter have small hinged shelves in front on which one can place food and drink. All the seats have good window-views. There is plenty of space on the roof luggage racks, and other floor space which one is surprised not to have been used for seating — but possibly the planners thought that many large rucksacks were going to be brought on to the train during the summer. In the luggage compartment space is allowed for four bicycles. The interior décor is pleasant, with the usual grey upholstery with red chevrons on the seats; each seat has retractable arm-rests; the floor is carpeted. One woman passenger, who I fancy did not travel by train very often, enquired when she got in whether it was a first class carriage. Ventilation is through top lights which pull downwards and inwards. The toilet was spacious and adapted for disabled persons; the door opened, closed and locked by pressing the appropriate buttons. The exterior doors are under the guard's control and slide open and shut like those on a London Underground train. The riding was much quieter than with Mark 1 stock and about the same as with Mark 2. The under-frame diesel motors were also quiet and caused no unpleasant vibration. Despite occasionally over-staying time at stations we kept the new schedule without difficulty.

One wonders how the units will cope with the summer traffic. I was told that present accommodation would then be doubled. A trolley refreshment service, which now operates over the Glasgow–Crianlarich section, will then come into use over the whole distance. One wonders whether, with more crowded trains, the single toilet in each pair of coaches will be enough. One has to wait and see. Meanwhile first impressions are favourable, both my own and those I have had from others. If they ever get as far as naming the units, as is now being done to HST power cars, I hope they will not forget John Anderson who, having no doubt turned in his grave when so much of the line was closed, would now rejoice to see this day.

The new Sprinter unit from Oban seen here at Crianlarich, awaiting the train from Fort William, in February 1989.   *Author*

The 12.35 service for Glasgow waiting to leave Oban in January 1989. *Author's collection*

The forecourt of the new station buildings at Oban (1989). *Author's collection*

Appendix One

Principal Bridges on the Line

While it was never necessary to construct a single tunnel, either on the main Callander and Oban line or along its two branches, a considerable number of large bridges had to be built. Most are still standing and many are still in use; of those from which the rails have been removed all but two may be safely used by pedestrians; one, indeed, has been made into a road bridge and carries a trunk road. The accompanying table lists them all. One, the most impressive structure, that across the mouth of Loch Etive near Connel, merits a more detailed description.

When it was completed in 1903 the bridge at Connel had a wider span than any rail bridge in the United Kingdom except the Forth Bridge. A single span was rendered necessary at this point because of the very rapid current which ran four times a day, twice in each direction corresponding with the tides, across the rapids of the Falls of Lora. It was therefore not possible to build any temporary staging across the waterway during construction. For this reason the cantilever pattern of structure was decided upon. There are two piers each at the water's edge on either side of the strait, and these take the thrust of the cantilever spans which depend from the tops of massive frames that direct the pressure obliquely downwards towards the piers which were made suitably massive. An inspection of a picture of the bridge will show better than any verbal description how its weight is taken. Between the two cantilever structures is a middle span of braced girders which was built out from either side to meet in the middle. Provision was made for expansion and contraction of the metal, by placing on the outer sides of each track rail, at the point where it passed from the cantilever to the centre span, of a "joint rail" close to the web, which curved gradually towards the centre of a three-inch gap, so that when a train passed across the outer part of each wheel flange was supported by the joint rail as it crossed the gap.

The bridge was high enough above the water to allow vessels to proceed beneath it, so that the railway had to be carried up a steep gradient from each side, along embankments leading to a three-arched masonry viaduct which gave on to the bridge itself. It was a single track, carried on jarrah-wood sleepers laid in the troughs of the steel rail-bearers and embedded in asphalt.

The bridge cost nearly £43,000 to build and required almost 2600 tons of steel. Before being brought into use it was tested by placing upon it a load many times greater than the usual weight of the trains that were to traverse it: eight locomotives, three locomotive tenders and many heavily-loaded mineral wagons were drawn up on it so that they occupied the track from end to end. It had been calculated that the centre of the bridge would then be depressed by three inches, and this was found to be the case when theodolites were trained upon it.

When the line finally closed the bridge itself was fortunately not just left to rust away, as is happening to its fellow across Loch Creran several miles to the north (though that it still in good condition and will be safe for walkers and cyclists for many years yet). The local authority took it over and has maintained it after adapting it for one-way road traffic controlled by lights at either end. Since it is the most impressive man-made object along the whole of the West Highland coast one cannot but approve, though it is sad that no trains rumble across it any more.

The massive cantilever bridge between Connel Ferry and North Connel across the seaward end of Loch Etive.   *Oakwood Collection*

The different style of girder bridge near Creagan, across the narrows of Loch Creran.   *Author*

Bridges on the Callander and Oban Railway

Situation	Description	Present Condition	Date Built	Contractor	Grid Reference
1. Crossed river in Pass of Leny obliquely from R. to L. bank about 2½ miles beyond Callander station.	Bowstring girder span with masonry abutments.	Ironwork removed: masonry remains.	1867	J. Mackay.	7087 2592
2. As above. but from L. to R. bank about 3 miles beyond Callander Station.	As above.	As above.	1867	As above.	7090 2587
3. Across Kendrum Burn about 1 mile beyond Balquhidder Junction Station	3 masonry arches.	In place but disused & much overgrown with vegetation below arches: walkable.	1869	As above.	7224 2575
4. Across narrow gully on W. side of Glen Ogle about 5 miles from Balquhidder Jc. Stn.	4 masonry arches.	In place but disused: walkable.	1869	As above.	7262 2572
5. Across wide gully on W. side of Glen Ogle about 5¼ miles from Balquhidder Jc. Stn.	12 masonry arches.	As above.	1869	As above.	7263 2571
6. Across Ardchyle Burn on S. side of Glen Dochart about ½ mile from Killin Jc. Stn.	3 masonry arches.	As above.	1871	Easton Gibb.	7283 2523
7. Across Ledcharrie Burn on S. side of Glen Dochart about 2 miles from Killin Jc. Stn.	3 masonry arches.	As above.	1871	As above.	7274 2507
8. Across burn on S. side of Strathfillan about 2½ miles beyond Crianlarich Stn.	3 masonry arches.	Used by trains.	1872	As above.	7275 2360
9. Across R. Fillan about 5 miles beyond Crianlarich Station.	3 masonry arches.	As above.	1873	As above.	7285 2334
10. Across Eas a ghaill Burn on S. side of Glen Lochy, about 9 miles beyond Tyndrum Stn.	6 masonry arches.	As above.	1877	J. MacKay.	7265 2210
11. Across R. Orchy near its outflow into Loch Awe about 2 miles beyond Dalmally Station.	7 girder spans on masonry piers.	As above.	1878	W. & T. Adams.	7281 2138
12. Across R. Awe, nearly 7 miles beyond Loch Awe Station.	3 girder spans on 2 intermediate masonry piers.	As above.	1879	As above.	7301 2029
13. Across R. Nant, ½ mile short of Taynuilt Station.	3 channel girder spans on concrete piers.	As above.	1885		7312 2008
14. Across R. Dochart, E. of village of Killin.	5 concrete arches on masonry piers.	In place, but disused: walkable	1885	John Best.	7326 2573
15 Across R. Lochay, just beyond Killin Station.	3 channel girder spans on concrete piers.	In place but disused: walkable.	1885	John Best.	7334 2575
16. Across narrows between Loch Etive & Firth of Lorne. ¼ mile N.W. of Connel Ferry Station.	Single cantilever span: (see text for details).	Now carries A828 trunk road: Oban–Ballachulish.	1898–1903	Arrol Bridge Coy.	7345 1911
17. Across narrows on Loch Creran ½ mile short of Creagan Station.	2 wide girder spans flanked on either side by a masonry arch.	In place, but disused: walkable.	1898–1903	As above.	7443 1978

Train ascending Glen Ogle and about to cross the 12-arch viaduct (*no. 5 in list on previous page*).   *Lens of Sutton*

The "facing-both ways" signals midway along "Anderson's Piano" (*above*) and at the eastern end of it (*below*). If a falling boulder broke a wire the signals went to the danger position. (*See Appendix 2 on opposite page.*)
                    Author's collection

Appendix Two

The Automatic Wire Safety Screen in the Pass of Brander

During the first year after the line had reached Oban, stones rolling down the side of Ben Cruachan in the region of the Pass of Brander began to be an annoyance and promised to be dangerous to passing trains. The company's first response was to set watchmen to patrol the endangered length of track, but this did not seem a sufficient protection, so, following a suggestion made by John Anderson in August 1881, the Engineer and Signal Department of the Caledonian Railway devised a contrivance which seemed likely to give maximum security.

Some 3 miles of line required to be covered. The mountain sloped to more than 3000 ft above it, and stones large and small were scattered over it. Some of them, dislodged by browsing sheep or from other causes, would from time to time, especially during the summer months, roll downwards, very likely disturbing others on their way. A stone might lodge on the track and cause a blockage into which a train might run; it might even strike a moving train. Some kind of fence seemed to be called for against which the falling boulder would either come to rest or, if the impact was so great that the fence was broken, would set off a warning device. (It would of course be possible for such a breakage to occur while a train was actually passing, but the resistance of the fence would at least have greatly lessened the stone's momentum and while it might still block the line it was not likely to do much damage to the train.)

It was decided to install an experimental length during the autumn of 1881. Four semaphore signal posts of the usual type, each with two signal arms which presented their faces in both directions, were erected in convenient positions so that enginedrivers on this section would always have one of them within sight in front. They covered a distance of about ⅝ mile, though they were not quite equidistant, being spaced to suit the ground. Along the line covered by these signals, to the north side of the track, a wire screen was placed, on average some 9 ft high, so that a stone of any considerable size would either strike the fence or, if it surmounted it, would clear the line altogether.

The fence wires were of steel and were fastened to the fence posts, which were also of steel, by staples that permitted free movement. If at any time a wire was broken by the impact of a falling boulder, the tension in it, which kept a signal weight arm on either side in the "proceed" position, would vanish, and the weight would drop, causing the signal arms on either side to move to "danger". When the screen was tested by the deliberate rolling of stones down the hill to strike it, it was found that some stones managed to get through without breaking a wire. The fence posts were then moved more closely together, at 6 yds instead of 12 yds intervals. A fresh test proved satisfactory, so the screen was then extended on either side of the experimental length to cover a distance of 3¼ miles. On 17th April, 1883 the completed scheme was brought into operation. It was fully automatic and required no signal boxes but only the presence of a single watchman who was based on a small hut where signal lamps and other stores were kept.

Locomotive drivers were instructed that if, along this stretch, they saw a signal at danger, they were to presume that a rock-fall had occurred and proceed cautiously at walking speed, sending the fireman forward to find out if an obstruction really were present. Once a clear signal could be seen ahead, or the last signal in the system had been passed, the fireman could re-join his companion on the footplate and the train could proceed normally.

An additional precaution was incorporated into the scheme; if on any of the rock slopes within the line cutting, on the track-side of the fence, there seemed the possibility of a fall, the rock at this point would be joined to the fence by a separate wire in such a manner that if it broke away and fell it would fracture a fence-wire, thus actuating the signals as a rock-fall from above would have done.

At the time of writing the fence has been operative for over a century and still gives satisfactory protection, though occasions when the signals are put to danger are few and far between.

Appendix Three
Mileages

	Miles	Opened	Closed		Miles	Opened	Closed
Callander	00·0	6/1870	9/1965	Killin Jct.	00·0	4/1886	9/1965
Strathyre	08·6	6/1870	9/1965	Killin	04·1	4/1886	9/1965
Kingshouse	10·7	6/1871	9/1965	Loch Tay	05·1	4/1886	1939
Balquhidder	11·7	6/1871	9/1965				
Glenoglehead	16·9	6/1870	9/1965				
Killin Jct.	19·1	4/1886	9/1965				
Luib	22·9	8/1873	9/1965	Connel Ferry	00·0		
Crianlarich[1]	28·9	8/1873	9/1965	North Connel	00·7	8/1903	3/1966
Tyndrum	34·1	8/1873		Benderloch		8/1903	3/1966
Dalmally	46·2	8/1877		Creagan		8/1903	3/1966
Loch Awe	48·8	7/1880	1965[2]	Appin		8/1903	3/1966
F. of Cruachan	52·0	10/1893	1965[3]	Duror		8/1903	3/1966
Taynuilt	57·9	7/1880		Kentallen		8/1903	3/1966
Ach-na-Cloich	60·4	7/1880	1965	Ballachulish Fy.	25·6	8/1903	3/1966
Connel Ferry	64·6	7/1880		Ballachulish	27·7	8/1903	3/1966
Oban	70·8	7/1880					

1. Trains ran from Crianlarich (Upper) to Oban after closure of Crianlarich (Lower).
2. Re-opened 1983 as unstaffed halt.
3. Re-opened 1987 as unstaffed halt on experimental basis.

Awe crossing

Courtesy, David and Charles

Appendix Four

Dimensions & Details of Steam Locomotives used on Callander & Oban Railway

Chief Dimensions & Details of Steam Locomotives used on Callander & Oban Railway:

Locomotive Type	2-4-2 Radial Tank	0-4-2 with 4-wheel tender	4-4-0 ("Oban Bogie I") with 4-wheel tender (later 6-wheel)	0-4-2 Saddle-tank	0-6-0 "Jumbo"	0-4-4 Tank	4-6-0 ("Oban Bogie II")	4-6-0 ("Oban Bogie III")	4-6-0 "Clan"	4-6-0 "Black Five"
Designer:	G. Brittain	B. Conner	G. Brittain	D. Drummond	D. Drummond	D. Drummond	J. MacIntosh	W. Pickersgill	C. Cumming	W. Stanier
Year of Manufacture:	1880	1878	1882	1885	1883	1883	1902	1922	1919	1934
Total heating Surface: sq.ft.	1091.5		1146.4 later 1090	684	1202.3	637.5	1905	1823	1467 + super-heat 256	1619 + super-heat 227
Firegrate Area: sq.ft.	13.4		14.4 later 17.0	10.23	19.5	14	20.63	21.9	25.5	27.8
Boiler Pressure: lb. sq. in.	130	140	130 later 150	140	150	150	175	185	175	225
Cylinders: inch.	2 outside 17½ × 22	2 outside 17½ × 24	2 outside 18 × 24	2 outside 14 × 20	2 inside 18 × 26	2 inside 16 × 22	2 inside 19 × 26	3 19½ × 26	2 outside 21 × 26	2 outside 18½ × 28
Wheel Diameter: (coupled)	5'8"	5'2"	5'2"	3'8"	5'0"	5'0"	5'0"	5'6"	6'0"	6'0"
Coupled Wheelbase:	8'0"	6'8¾"	8'5"	7'0"	6'3"	6'4"	11'3"	12'3"	12'10"	15'0"
Total Wheelbase:	21'0"	14'0"	21'0"	20'6"	16'3"	21'4"	24'9"	24'9"	24'7"	27'2"
Weight of engine in workg. order: (in tons)	51.6	34.6	41.6 later 40.85	31.2	41.25	37.75	57.4	62.8	62.3	74.0
Weight of tender in workg. order: (in tons)		24.0	24.0		34.0		37.2	37.9	42.0	52.0
Adhesion weight: (in tons)	29.7		27.5	25.7	41.25	25.0	42.7	45.7	45.5	54.0
Water capacity (in gallons)	1200	1550	1550 later 1840	800	2840	830	3000	3000	3000	4000
Coal capacity (in tons)	3	4	4 later 4¼	1¼	4½	1¼	4½	4½	5	9
Tractive effort (at 85% boiler pr.)	10950	13310	13860	10600	17901	11960	23269	23555	23650	25455

Appendix Five

Principal Events on the Callander and Oban Railway

Date:

22/6/1864 First meeting of Callander and Oban Railway Committee in Glasgow.

5/7/1865 Callander and Oban Railway Act passed.

1/9/1865 Appointment of John Anderson as the Company's Secretary.

27/6/1866 J. McKay given contract for construction of Callander–Glenoglehead section.

1/6/1870 Callander–Killin (Glenoglehead) section opened.

8/1873 Killin (Glenoglehead)–Tyndrum section opened.

1/5/1877 Tyndrum–Dalmally section opened.

30/6/1880 Ceremonial opening of whole line from Callander at Oban.

20/6/1881 Steamer services on Loch Etive begin from Ach-na-Cloich pier.

27/6/1882 Building of safety fence against falling boulders in P. of Brander authorised.

1/4/1886 Killin and Loch Tay branch from Killin Junction opened.

20/12/1894 Spur line opened from Crianlarich Junction to Crianlarich Upper Station on West Highland line.

7/8/1896 Callander and Oban Railway (Ballachulish Extension) Act passed.

4/3/1903 Authorisation of enlargement of Oban station.

7/7/1905 Introduction of "C. & O. Hotel Express".

31/7/1907 Retirement of John Anderson after 42 years' service on the C. & O.

1/7/1909 Rail-bus service, Connel Ferry–North Connel, begins to operate.

22/6/1914 Connel Ferry adapted for use by road vehicles and pedestrians.

3/8/1914 Introduction of Pullman Observation Car *Maid of Morven* on Glasgow–Oban workings. (Discontinued February 1915, reinstated March 1919).

9/9/1939 Trains ceased to run between Killin and Loch Tay.

27/9/1965 Landslide in Glen Ogle permanently blocks service between Callander and Crianlarich.

26/3/1966 Ballachulish branch closed.

23/1/1989 Sprinters replace locomotive-hauled trains on Oban branch of West Highland line.

Bibliography

The Callander & Oban Railway: John Thomas.
The Caledonian Railway: O. S. Nock.
Scottish Locomotive History: 1831–1923: Campbell Highet.
Forty Years of Caledonian Locomotives: 1882–1922: H. J. Campbell Cornwell.
"Rambles on the Caledonian Railway": G. W. J. Potter. *Railway Magazine* (August & September 1912).
"The Callander & Oban Railway": J. F. Gairns. *Railway Magazine* (July 1923).
"The Callander & Oban Section of the LMSR": O. S. Nock. *Railway Magazine* (January 1938).

Acknowledgements

My thanks are due, firstly to my publishers for advice and co-operation in selecting suitable illustrations; secondly to British Rail for comfortably carrying me on the Callander and Oban Railway and (subsequently to 1965/6) on the Oban branch of the West Highland Line more times than I can remember; thirdly to my friends John Ransom and Canon Brian Simpson who have given me advice and material; finally to the staff of the Scottish Record Office, Edinburgh, who kindly gave me facilities for research in their archives.

Index

Accidents:
 Dalmally 1886   149, 151
 P. of Brander 1881   149
 Strathyre 1883   149
Anderson, John   17–25, 27–30, 73, 82, 84, 89
Argyll, Duke of   17, 95
Blane Valley Rly   13–14
Breadalbane, Marquess of   17, 27, 75, 77
C & O Hotel Express   133
Caledonian Rly   14–15, 17–20, 24, 26, 71, 76–77, 85, 90, 92, 98, 115, 123, 130, 135, 150,154, 172

Campbell, Sir D.   18
Closures of lines   136–137, 155–156
Connel Bridge   63, 113, 137, 169
Contractors:
 Adams, W. & T.   27
 Best, J.   82, 96
 Easton Gibb   24
 Ireland & Co.   27
 McDonald of Skye   77
 McKay, J.   18–19,25
Creagan Bridge   113, 169
Derailment 1881   151
Dunblane, Doune & Callander Rly   13, 65

Edinburgh & Glasgow Rly   14, 17
Fire on train 1948   152
Forth & Clyde Junc. Rly   13–14
Glasgow & South Western Rly   29
Gradient profile   16
Highland Rly   75, 91, 95
Inspectors, B.O.T.:
   Hutchinson   149
   Marindin   151
   Tyler   20–21
Inveraray branch (proposed)   95
Locomotives
   2–4–2T (Brittain)   115, 151, 173
   2–4–2T (Webb)   115
   0–4–2 (Conner)   115, 151, 173
   4–4–0 (Brittain)   115, 117, 122,
      173
   0–4–2ST (Drummond)   122, 173
   0–6–0 (Drummond)   122, 173
   4–6–0 (McIntosh)   123, 173
   0–4–4T (Drummond)   123, 173
   "Connel Bus"   123
   4–6–0 (Pickersgill)   127–128, 173
   4–6–0 "Clan" (Cumming)
      127–128, 173
   4–6–0 (Stanier)   8, 40, 128, 173
London & North Western Rly   27, 29
McCaig, J.   28
McGregor, Sir M.   18–19, 31
Nant Bridge, destruction of   150
North British Rly   14, 25, 84, 89
Pullman Dining Cars   130
Pullman Observation Cars
   129–131, 134
Royal Scotsman luxury train   163
Safety Fence ("Anderson's Piano")
   73, 163, 171
Scottish Central Rly   13–14, 17, 64
Sleeping Cars   130–121, 136
Snow Blockage 1947   152
Sprinters   164–165

Stations:
   Ach-na-Cloich   63, 70, 161, 172
   Appin   113–114, 172
   Ballachulish   7, 70, 96, 114, 137,
      172
   Ballachulish Ferry   114, 172
   Balquhidder Junc.   19–20, 31,
      67, 172
   Benderloch   7, 113, 172
   Callander   20, 24–25, 31, 65,
      133, 151–152, 172
   Connel Ferry   63, 70, 96, 172
   Creagan   113, 172
   Crianlarich Lower   7, 24, 40,
      67–68, 95, 172
   Crianlarich Upper   7, 67, 72,
      92, 162, 172
   Dalmally   25, 27, 50, 68, 172
   Duror   113–114, 172
   Falls of Cruachan   68, 172
   Glenoglehead   20, 40, 77
   Kentallen   114, 156, 172
   Killin   7, 67, 82, 84, 136–137,
      172
   Killin Junc.   7, 40, 67, 82,
      136–137, 172
   Kingshouse   31, 67, 172
   Loch Awe   27, 68, 161, 172
   Loch Tay   84, 136–137, 172
   Luib   24, 40, 68, 172
   Oban   29–30, 70, 72, 97, 133
      156, 172
   Strathyre   20–21, 23, 31, 65, 172
   Taynuilt   27, 70, 172
   Tyndrum   19, 24–25, 50, 68, 172
Timetables   23, 132, 135, 139–148,
   162, 164
Trossachs branch (proposed)   84,
   89
West Highland Rly   40, 50, 91–92,
   95–96